Dee Beard Dean

A PAINTER BY PROVIDENCE

Dee Beard Dean

A PAINTER BY PROVIDENCE

WRITTEN BY MICHELLE MORTON

Morton Arts Media
Greensboro, North Carolina

Dee Beard Dean
A Painter by Providence

All rights reserved.
No part of this publication may be reproduced or transmitted in any form or by any means, electronic or mechanical, including photography, photocopying, recording or any other information storage and retrieval system without prior permission in writing from the publisher.

© 2010 Morton Arts Media, LLC
1814 Madison Avenue
Greensboro, North Carolina 27403
Tel: 336.312.8264
E-mail: michelle@mortonartsmedia.com
Website: mortonartsmedia.com

All photographs of artwork © 2010 Dee Beard Dean
ISBN-13: 978-0-9796868-1-8
ISBN-10: 0-979-6868-1-4

Library of Congress Control Number: 2010903953

For information on artworks by Dee Beard Dean or to order the book,
E-mail: deebearddean@mac.com
Website: deebearddean.com

Cover Design: Eileen McFalls
Interior Design: Michelle Morton, Eileen McFalls
Copy Editing: Janet Tucker
Photos of Dee Beard Dean by Nick Chalfa
Front Cover and Title Page Artwork: *Bouganvilla and Boat,* oil on canvas, 16 x 20 inches
Back Cover Artwork: *Springtime Renewal*, oil on canvas, 11 x 14 inches
Printed in the U.S. by The R. L. Bryan Company, Columbia, SC

dedication

I owe the early nourishment of my art career to my mother whose artistic spirit encouraged me all my life. I also acknowledge my late husband, David Dean, for his encouragement and never-ending support of my art career. With his help, I was able to paint the miles of canvas that established my art career.

    I dedicate this book to my wonderful husband, Dr. Nicolai Chalfa who calls himself my "art slave." Since retirement from his medical career he takes care of the day-to-day tasks, which enables me to do what I love—paint! Our mutual passion for travel has helped me to broaden my artistic horizons and his constant love and devotion have given me the inspiration—not only for painting—but also for doing this book.

    I also dedicate the book to my two children, Terry Beard Sargent and John Beard, both of whom have inherited my love for art and are emerging artists themselves.

    Lastly and above all, I thank God for the talent He has given me, the many blessings I have had in this life, and for the many friends I have made along the way. I hope that the joy and excitement that I experienced in creating these paintings will be shared by you, the viewer.

—Dee Beard Dean

Cortona in the Morning
oil on canvas
40 x 30 inches

table of contents

foreword	13
by Clayton Bass	
a painter by providence	21
daydreams on driftwood	39
drawn to design	55
the substance of soul	69
a kaleidoscope of colors	83
seeing the splendor	101
the beauty of plein air painting	119
by Dee Beard Dean	
studies and quick sketches	123
the allure of light	133
ambassadors of art	155
index	171

Dee Beard Dean

Acropolis, Porch of the Maidens
oil on canvas
20 x 24 inches

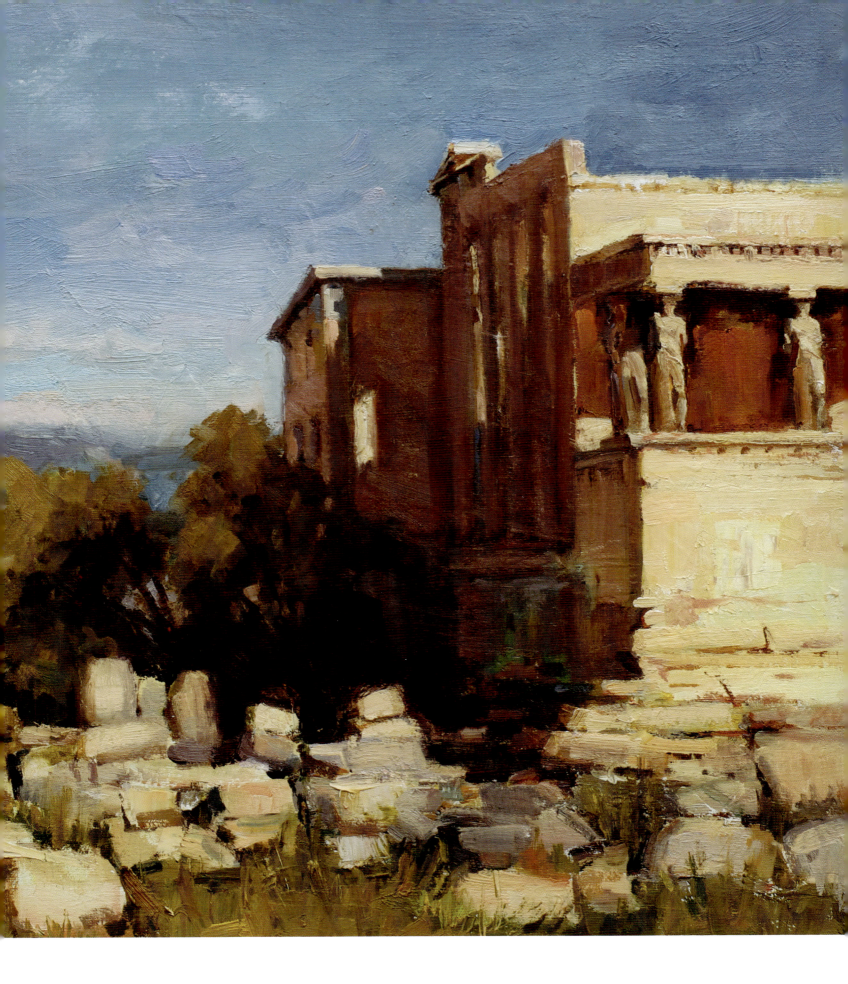

Dee Beard Dean

Sunset Grandeur
oil on canvas
24 x 30 inches

foreword by clayton bass

You are very fortunate to be holding this book in your hand. As the title states, providence is involved, and yes, it also applies to you. What motivated you to pick up the book? You may recognize the artist's name on the cover, or have found the colorful cover image impossible to pass up. But what you hold is a ticket, an opportunity to take a journey through the life of a true Renaissance woman.

Hers is a life with the same potential limitations and opportunities we all face. Yet, she is propelled by imagination and a passion to develop and refine her diverse talents and skills. Dee's journey becomes an impassioned one due to her keen, inquisitive nature, a willingness to follow her heart, and her love of nature, light, and color. Come along on her journey and you will witness the birth and growth of an artist, a true student of life.

I encourage you to consider this book, the ticket in your hand, as an opportunity that can inform and inspire your own life's journey. In so many ways, Dee's story is a universal one, and as told here, has the power to inspire, and shape your perception about believing in yourself, taking risks and recognizing opportunities. Her story is one of personal transformation, a potential we all share. Look closely at her paintings, and see how they form an unfolding journal of her vivid experiences, rarely grand, but rich in simplicity of subject and place. The result of Dee's imagination compels you to look more closely at the profound beauty of everyday life. When you take the time to really look and see, the immense beauty will amaze you.

For Dee Beard Dean, her early years in Indiana were the perfect setting to inspire a young girl to become attuned to nature. These early experiences nourished her and provided a lifetime of rich memories and reverence for the natural order of the world. As her journey progressed, the joy and obligations of becoming a wife and mother shifted her focus to the essential needs of those she loved and cared for. Her husband's work transported the family to a new life in South Florida, into a tropical, lush environment, quite alien to her previous experiences. These new colorful vistas broadened her view of the world and sparked a fresh wave of creative ideas.

Dee's creative journey progressed quickly from delicate paintings on driftwood, in bountiful supply, to the more sophisticated pursuits of fashion design. With a keen eye for style and strong seamstress skills, combined with a flair for marketing, Dee transformed her label, *Dee Beard Collections*, into one of Florida's most sought after fashion lines. The media came calling, and soon Dee was in great demand, and running a fashion empire.

Amid the pressures of nurturing an expanding business, she never lost sight of nurturing her son and daughter, and encouraging their own creative development. Both are now professional artists, and share their mother's passion for nature and capturing its wonders within their own works.

The allure of art making as a primary focus eventually led Dee to apprentice with one of Florida's most acclaimed portrait artists, and demand for Dee's accomplished works grew steadily. Dee's ability to bond with and understand her subjects helped to imbue an authenticity within each portrait. In time, Dee was in demand to teach workshops and in doing so she discovered a marvelous thing. The more she taught, the more she learned. She was a natural, enthusiastic teacher who loved to see her students grow as artists. Teaching was another way for her to share her skills, experience and life's journey with others, and the benefits were mutual.

During the past decade Dee has become known as one of the most respected *plein air* painters in the U.S. Her masterful brushstrokes and sensitive color palette have a way of transforming each image into a personal vision that is vibrant, joyful, and a celebration of its subject. Within her realms of light, shadow, color and texture, she leaves room for you, the viewer, to add your own memories and imagination, thereby completing the work.

In her extensive travels Dee realized how many excellent Southeastern artists were unknown beyond the region. Her genuine desire to enhance their recognition and build a strong sense of community among artists led to the formation of the organization Plein Air Painters of the Southeast. The group's reputation for excellence continues to spread through their annual exhibitions, workshops and through these artists' efforts to champion the fresh approach of painting outside with nature as the ultimate resource and inspiration.

Dee's journey is ongoing, and now she has other kindred spirits who are blazing a trail together. Ever mindful of the traditions they honor through their work, they are committed to bringing new energy to the impressionist painting tradition. With this book, you can join Dee on her journey, and grow from the experience. Whatever your personal interest or profession may be, from the story and paintings that follow you will gain a fresh perspective and appreciation for the new day that dawns tomorrow. Indeed, providence is a wonderful thing.

Clayton Bass, *President and CEO*
Huntsville Museum of Art

DEE BEARD DEAN

On the Road to San Miguel
oil on canvas
16 x 20 inches

A Painter By Providence

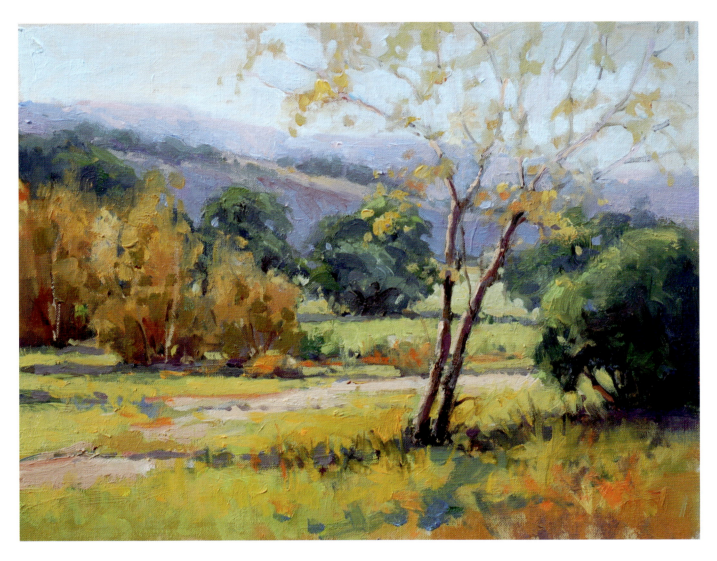

The Beginning of Spring
oil on canvas
11 x 14 inches

DEE BEARD DEAN

The Last Blooms
oil on canvas
15 x 30 inches

A Painter By Providence

Dee Beard Dean

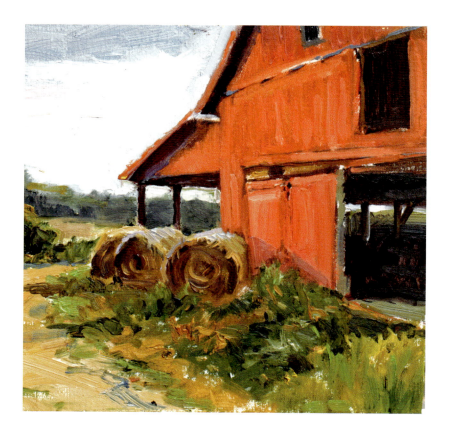

Hay Barn
oil on canvas
12 x 12 inches

*Sunset on
the Marsh*
oil on canvas
30 x 40 inches

a painter by providence

    Some lives appear committed to an artistic path long before social or academic expectations begin to seize the imagination of youth. Inspired by their strong inner vision, born artists tend to view the world unlike others. To their penetrating eyes, the shapes, the hues and patterns of things are simply colored by a light more exquisite and luminous than that which most people are able to see.

    Dee Beard Dean is an acclaimed modern day painter who has always possessed this rare and irrepressible capacity to grasp the beauty of the world, and to this aim, she has remained devoted her entire life. As a child, her freehand sketches and intuitive eye for color and detail were precocious, but Dee also possessed a self-discipline and bold determination that took everyone in her tiny Midwestern hometown by surprise.

    Her childhood provided few of the societal advantages or influences one might expect a successful artist to have enjoyed as a youngster. Art galleries did not exist in her community and the local high school offered no classes in art. She and her high school classmates, seven in all, were taught strictly in the basics of academic curriculum. So, to appreciate Dee's work, one has to also appreciate her tenacious willpower, her boundless creative energy, and the fortunate occurrence of people who were present at different stages in her life to encourage and teach her.

Dee's artistic journey began with the wholehearted encouragement of her mother who found every opportunity she could to nurture her children's creative imaginations. Dee and her four siblings grew up in rural Indiana, in an Amish community defined by quiet streets lined with clean, modest clapboard houses and backyard vegetable gardens. The surrounding countryside was a bucolic patchwork of crop fields and family-owned farmsteads. Dee Beard Dean was born Dolores Barker and she was the eldest of her four siblings: Bonnie, Don, Jerry and Jim. From grammar school on, Dee was known around her hometown as the "art girl," which is to say, the person everyone went to when an artist was needed to illustrate a flyer, bulletin board, poster or banner.

Despite the lack of galleries or art curriculum in her hometown, it would be inaccurate to say Dee lacked artistic influence during her formative years. Sometimes, the learning process simply takes place not in a classroom, but deep in the day-to-day consciousness. Looking back, Dee realizes how her perceptions about art were gradually assimilated from the land, from the people with whom she grew up, and from simple childhood pastimes like picking blackberries in summer, or listening to the muted stillness of an apple orchard, save for the intermittent buzzing of bees among the treetops.

It was the ordinary, everyday minutia of details and observations that sparked Dee's curiosity and opened her mind to the powerful beauty of nature. The black, fertile "muck" fields that produced crops and garden vegetables to feed the families of her hometown also provided ample nourishment for Dee's budding artistic spirit. The lyrical patterns of corn rows and the pockets of verdant forests, the rhythm of life played out in perfect harmony with the seasons, and the friendliness of folks who

A Painter By Providence

Fall Serenity
oil on canvas
16 x 20 inches

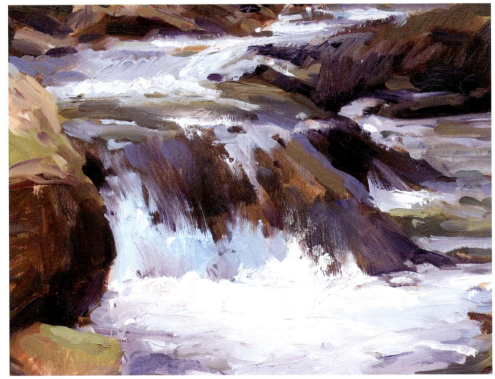

River Rapids
oil on canvas
16 x 20 inches

Dee Beard Dean

Tidal Creek
oil on canvas
30 x 40 inches

A Painter By Providence

depended upon each other in good times and bad; these offered a nearly idyllic environment for a child with a prolific imagination to thrive.

Information about classical art in Dee's hometown may have been scarce, but her community was rich in traditional handmade craftsmanship. The Amish boys were schooled in the intricacies of furniture making, carving beautiful pieces of fine furniture. The girls infused creativity into almost every domestic chore, producing gorgeous needlework fabrics and jars of picture-perfect homegrown vegetables, which they canned throughout the summer.

Like Dee, her mother also possessed the heart and mind of an artist whose medium and tools were not canvas and paintbrush, but rather yards of colorful cloth and a sewing machine. Her mother could sew gorgeous silk and taffeta dresses for her daughters using patterns she designed and cut herself. Consequently, Dee and her sister Bonnie were often admired for their fashionable wardrobe.

Sewing clothes was one way young women in rural Indiana prepared for adulthood, but to Dee, sewing was more than just a life skill. She found working with her hands and creating smart, functional clothing to be an enjoyable and rewarding hobby. Because her mother set high standards in sewing—making Dee rip out seams over and over until she got it right—Dee acquired a sharp attention for detail. With practice, she learned to turn weak frustration into steely determination, and mustered the patience for undoing and redoing her work until the seams were perfectly straight and smooth. These simple lessons, wrought from countless hours working a sewing machine, instilled in Dee a tireless work ethic. And, though no one knew it at the time, her sewing skills would eventually open doors to unimaginable career opportunities.

A Painter By Providence

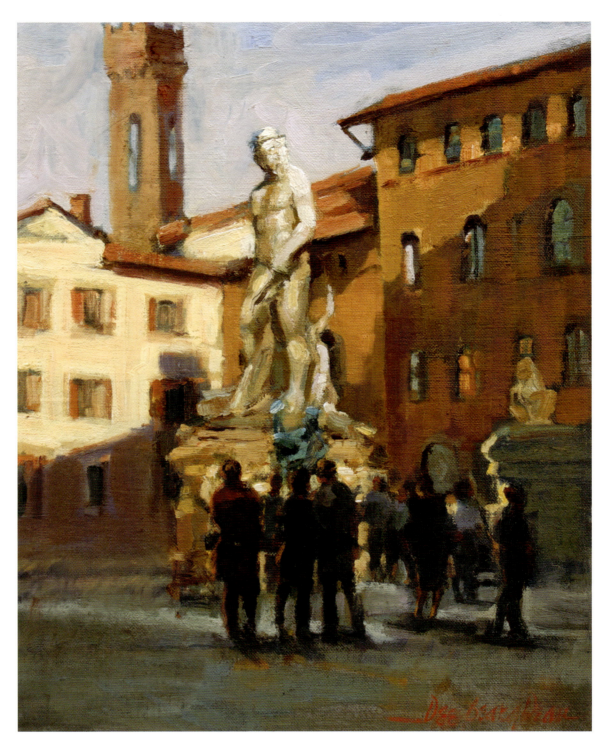

Admiring Neptune
oil on canvas
14 x 11 inches

Dee Beard Dean

River Dance
oil on canvas
30 x 24 inches

It was fortunate for Dee that her mother nurtured her artistic yearnings. Yet, while Dee feels grateful for her early influences, she also acknowledges that her artistic drive was so strong right from the beginning, it would have found expression even in a vacuum. "If I had been stranded on an deserted island as a child," says Dee, "I would have picked up a stick to draw in the sand."

In the debate of nature versus nurture regarding artistic aptitude, Dee remembers one particular incident suggesting how both influences are essential. Dee vividly recalls the defining moment when she first realized her love of drawing was actually a prized gift. At a very young age, Dee, in a fit of creativity, took a crayon to some newly hung wallpaper in her parent's bedroom. To the young artist, the wallpaper seemed the perfect ground for making pictures, and Dee happily drew a pair of little girls representing her best friends. The figures, unlike stick figures rendered by most children her age, were rounded out portraits of pigtailed girls holding hands, detailed with colorful hair bows and ruffled dresses.

Her father came home that night, saw the drawings and angrily called his wife to the bedroom to "see what her daughter had done." When Dee's mother saw the pictures, her reaction was quite the opposite. Eyes beaming with pride, her mother clasped her hands and exclaimed, "How *beautiful!*"

It was Dee's first realization that art had value beyond mere child's play. Her mother's reaction of delight and appreciation for the primitive drawings left an indelible impression in Dee's psyche, molding the young child's personality with a love of creative self-expression.

To encourage her daughter's talent, Dee's mother rolled the leftover wallpaper out on the kitchen floor so Dee could draw on it to her heart's content. A few years later, recognizing that her daughter needed a more formal education in art, Dee's mother bought Dee a professional artist's paint set and sent away for a mail order course titled the "Famous Artists School" advertised in the back pages of Good Housekeeping magazine. With the headline declaring, "We're looking for a few people who like to draw," the magazine advertisement offered to critique works for artists who could first pass a drawing aptitude test. Dee passed the "test" and eagerly turned in the assignments, which were then sent back to her with a grade. Though hardly a substitute for formal studio instruction, this mail order course did introduce Dee to some of the rudimentary academic principles of art such as color theory, perspective and composition.

As a young teen, Dee was offered her first commission to paint a mural on her Aunt Samantha's wall. It was substantial money for someone her age, but more importantly, it sparked the idea that this gift she possessed had three benefits: First, creating art was immensely self-satisfying; second, it seemed to delight the people for whom she created the art; third, and most surprising of all, it could actually provide a source of income. With these realizations in mind, Dee began to dream of attending art school after graduation to study to become a professional artist.

It was a life goal wholly inconsistent with the traditional expectations for a young woman from Indiana, but it wasn't the first time Dee toyed with the idea of becoming a professional artist. In the seventh grade, she recalls a particular assignment her teacher gave in which the students were to write an essay about their aspirations after high school. Dee wrote about the things that most interested her and, as she stood in front of the room reading her essay, her ideas were met with snickers from some of her classmates. To Dee's peers—and to many of the grown-ups in her community—her desire to work as a fashion designer or fine artist seemed quite odd.

A Painter By Providence

Hideaway
oil on canvas
14 x 11 inches

Stroll Through the Market
oil on canvas
24 x 20 inches

A Painter By Providence

The Road to Home
oil on canvas
16 x 20 inches

Art was an admirable talent, yes, but utterly inconceivable as a career choice.

The lack of encouragement to pursue art as a profession did nothing, however, to discourage her. After graduation, Dee attended the Kendall School of Art and Design in Grand Rapids, Michigan. At the Kendall School, Dee thrived in the company of like-minded students. Belonging to this community of fellow artists emboldened Dee's creative spirit and began to give substance and shape to her childhood dreams.

Dee Beard Dean

Rio Grande Spring
oil on canvas
20 x 24 inches

Overlooking the Gorge
oil on canvas
16 x 20 inches

A Painter By Providence

Rio Pueblo Gorge
oil on canvas
16 x 12 inches

Dee Beard Dean

San Juan Llano
oil on canvas
16 x 20 inches

Crashing Waves
oil on canvas
11 x 14 inches

Dee Beard Dean

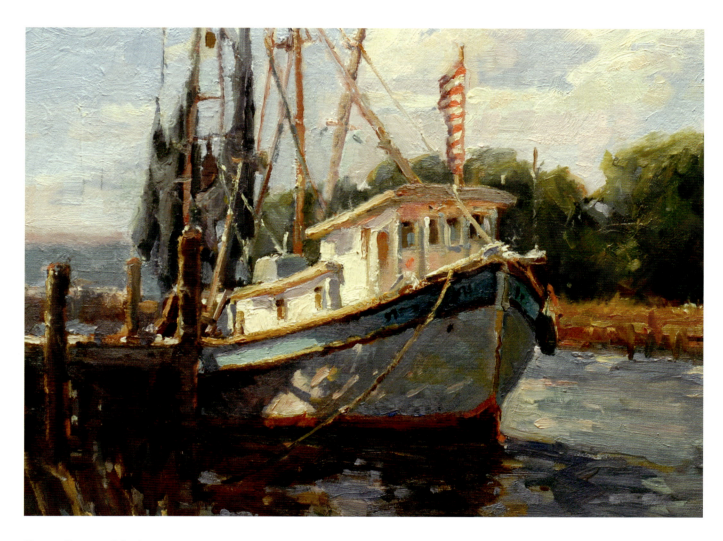

East Coast Shrimper
oil on canvas
16 x 20 inches

daydreams on driftwood

Eventually, Dee married and had two children, Teresa (Terry) and John. For a time, she slipped into the traditional role of wife and mother, putting her dreams of an art career on hold to take care of her family. In 1970, a job opportunity for her husband came up in Tavernier, Florida and the family made plans to head south. To a Midwestern girl, the thought of relocating to the Florida Keys was a bit outlandish, and at first, Dee was skeptical. In hindsight, however, moving her family to Florida proved one of the most fateful turning points in her life.

The family moved into a house on the water overlooking the mangrove islands dotting Florida Bay. Her closest neighbors were a troop of feral spider monkeys living among the gumbo limbo trees and live oaks surrounding their home. Once, when she left the house to pick up her aunt from the airport, they returned to find that the door to the house had been left open. Stepping inside, they discovered that the monkeys had invited themselves in and were, quite literally, swinging from the chandelier: the countertops and floor were strewn with banana peels and empty paper cupcake molds.

Such Robinson Crusoesque anecdotes became almost commonplace for Dee and her family as they settled into this tropical paradise, worlds away from the throbbing beat of Miami's city life just 60 miles to the north.

The laid-back pace of the Keys allowed Dee time to explore and innovate new activities to engage her children's curiosity about the region's natural wonders. She and her two young children found ever-intriguing playgrounds among the shallow coral reefs, the mangrove islands and shell-strewn beaches.

One day, while picking up sculpted pieces of driftwood that had washed up on shore, Dee imagined how the distressed wood might look with scenes of local wildlife and various marine subjects painted on it. After painting a few pieces of driftwood, a friend who owned an art gallery saw Dee's artwork and offered to sell the pieces in her gallery. It was this chance opportunity that marked the beginning of Dee's career as a professional artist. Visitors to the Keys loved the driftwood art and

it wasn't uncommon for collectors to drive down from Miami or Ft. Lauderdale specifically to pick up more driftwood paintings by Dee.

About the same time, her children, Terry and John, had discovered their own way to create interesting works of art from found objects. On a summer's whim, Terry and John began collecting beautiful sand-washed rocks along the beach, which they painted to look like "rock people." The gallery owner representing Dee's driftwood paintings found the little rock people delightful and offered to sell them in her shop as well. Quickly, the rock people became collector items, virtually flying out of the gallery door as soon as they arrived.

Today, both Terry and John are professional artists living in North Carolina and Florida, respectively. Their early success painting and marketing their works in the Florida Keys enlivened their careers and artworks with confidence and gave them a professional edge few budding artists enjoy at such an early age.

Grounded
oil on canvas
15 x 30 inches

A Painter By Providence

Wading Spoonbills
oil on canvas
12 x 15 inches

As the Beard family's art business boomed, Dee's watercolor landscapes and driftwood paintings soon attracted the attention of Peggy Merrick, a well-known portrait artist from Marathon, Florida. The artist offered Dee her first mentorship in portraiture and, after studying as Merrick's protégé, Dee was busy with commissioned portraits of her own.

Like any self-respecting artist, Dee lived, for a time, a Bohemian dream. The years spent beachcombing and painting watercolors and seascapes on driftwood, while raising children in the relaxed, casual atmosphere of the Keys deepened Dee's creative vision.

Living immersed in the Old Conch culture of the Florida Keys with its endless adventures in boating, fishing and diving the coral reefs, and its kaleidoscope of tropical hues, forever colored Dee's perspective on life. The turquoise blue bays, the whimsical coconut palm trees and the prolific crimson bougainvillea, growing in beds of coral rock like roadside weeds, all provided daily sensations for the eyes.

Garden Pampering (LEFT)
oil on canvas
30 x 24 inches

Dee Beard Dean

Grampa's Truck
oil on canvas
11 x 14 inches

Laguna Mist
oil on canvas
11 x 14 inches

Sunflowers and Seashell (RIGHT)
oil on canvas
24 x 20 inches

Like the fertile fields of rural Indiana, this was a place in which the creative spirit could flourish and cascade over every boundary of the imagination. Unlike Dee's home state, however, the beauty of this landscape was as peculiar as it was extravagant.

In this watery universe with its splashy colors and lavish textures, life assumed unconventional forms—lacy sea fans, whorled shells, eccentric coral formations—even the birds were oddly shaped. And pink was everywhere you looked, from the derelict Key Largo shanties along US-1, to the ubiquitous conch shells perched atop cinder block walls, to the flocks of roseate spoonbills that would descend every winter on the mangrove swamps to feed on microscopic pink shrimp.

Today, Dee is known for her colorful, impressionistic palette and it's easy to imagine where her tastes and artistry for bright pigments and sparkling sunlight first took root in her imagination. Years of intense tropical sunlight, and the sweet memories of hours spent with her children collecting and painting artifacts washed up on the beaches continue to influence her creative tastes.

The sunbathed culture of the Florida Keys imbued Dee with a love for the unfamiliar such that today, whether painting a Tuscan hamlet or Ecuadorian villagescape, her brushstrokes speak of a sense of unfettered freedom and of an infinite capacity to revel in the glory and richness of every moment.

DEE BEARD DEAN

The Adjustment
oil on canvas
30 x 24 inches

Marsh Sunset
oil on canvas
20 x 16 inches

Dee Beard Dean

Laguna Beach
oil on canvas
11 x 14 inches

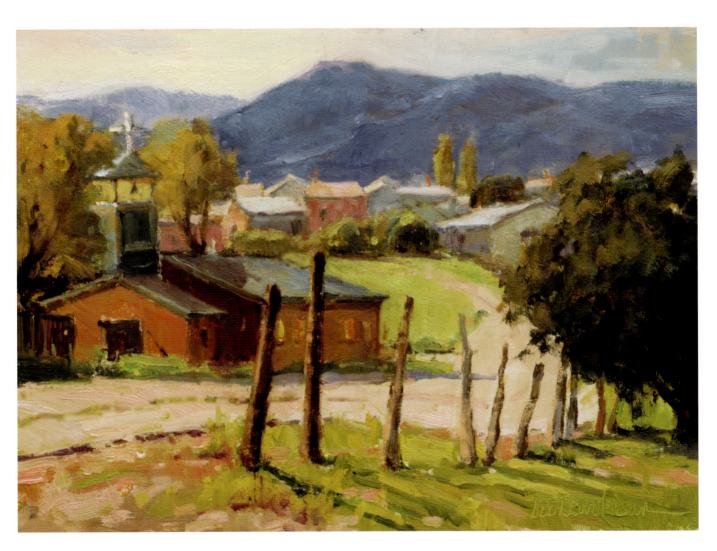

Truchas Morning
oil on canvas
12 x 16 inches

Dee Beard Dean

Rolling Hills
oil on canvas
20 x 24 inches

A Painter By Providence

Low Tide
oil on canvas
16 x 20 inches

DEE BEARD DEAN

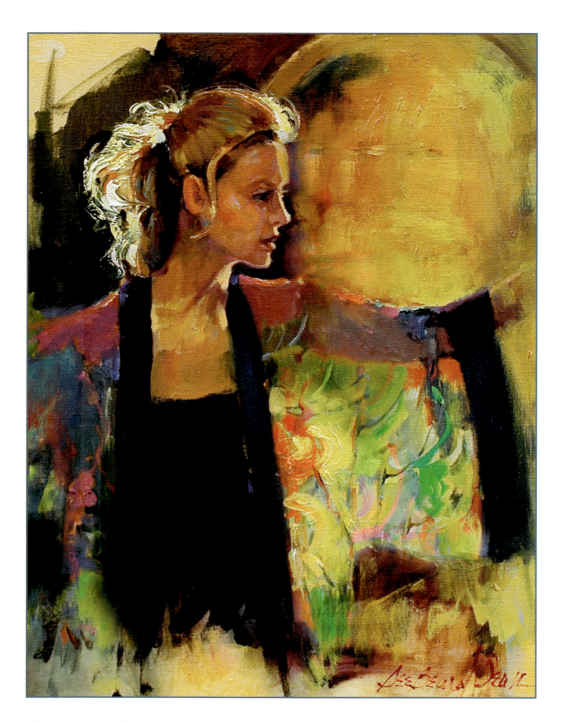

The Backlit Painter
oil on canvas
20 x 16 inches

drawn to design

The decade Dee spent raising her family in the Florida Keys became a mosaic of treasured memories after a business opportunity prompted Dee and her husband to relocate to Ft. Myers, Florida, in 1980. This quaint old Florida community is flanked by the vast Everglades sawgrass ecosystem to the east and the famed white beaches of the Gulf Coast to the west. As her children were growing into their own lives of independence, Dee decided to turn her energies from homemaker, part-time painter and full-time mother to the world of business and retail marketing.

Dee had a lifelong interest in fashion and design and, with a little sales experience acquired from working in a dress boutique years ago, she decided to open a clothing store in downtown Ft. Myers. Soon after opening the doors of "Dee's Boutique," she began to realize the wide-open market opportunities for fashionable designer wear in this sizzling little city with its winter influx of stylish sun lovers from the North.

Dee had never lacked for a sense of adventure, but finding the courage to run her own dress shop was another matter. She recalls, "How frightened I was at my first fashion market in Miami where I had to purchase thousands of dollars worth of inventory. Luckily, the choices I made sold well, and that gave me the courage to keep going back for more." The success of her first store eventually led to other store locations throughout Florida.

Her clothing boutiques specialized in European designs, and introduced for the first time in the Ft. Myers market, clothing with a sophisticated, international flair. Customers eagerly sought the labels she carried and Dee soon began experimenting with designing her own line of women's sportswear. The sewing and pattern making skills she learned early in life gave Dee a savvy and inventive skill for choosing fabrics, cutting patterns to make prototype pieces and developing her own unique line of clothing.

Breaking into the glamorous world of fashion design is the providence of only a lucky and talented few. Typically, clothing designers possess hands trained for illustration and a keen eye for design, but to experiment with prototype pieces or to manufacture garments, they must rely on a stable of patternmakers and sewers.

Like other accomplished designers, Dee too had an exquisite eye for good taste and trend-setting style. And her drawing skills enabled her to turn pen-and-ink sketches into 3-D skirts and tops flowing with color and texture. But it was her sewing and patternmaking skills that gave Dee a unique edge for breaking into in this fiercely competitive field.

A Painter By Providence

Ponte Vecchio at Sunset
oil on canvas
24 x 36 inches

Because of her early years spent as an accomplished seamstress, Dee could sketch her garment designs, and also act as patternmaker and finally as seamstress, constructing the whole garment from beginning to end. With these skills, Dee's retail boutiques became her testing grounds to market her unique designs and apparel label. The "Dee Beard Collections" proved as popular with her clientele as the well-known designer wear her stores sold. As Dee's line of clothing developed a following, first with her own retail customers, her label eventually spread far beyond the window displays of her clothing stores in Florida.

Dee's designer collections of sportswear were characterized by her innovative use of asymmetrical hemlines, harmonious color palettes and contrasting materials such as silks and soft leather. When the sales for her line reached a critical point, Dee bought out a cut-and-sew manufacturer in Orlando and began mass-producing her line with its seasonal Spring, Summer, Fall, Cruise, and Winter collections. She conducted runway shows of her label five times a year in the major fashion merchandise marts of Miami, Dallas, Los Angeles, New York and Atlanta. At the height of her career in fashion design, Dee was selling her label and clothing line to 450 luxury retail clothing stores across America from Beverly Hills, California to Worth Avenue in Palm Beach as well as several boutiques in South America.

To supply the stores carrying her label, Dee's company would begin the process of creating a seasonal collection line using countless bolts of "gray goods." These bolts of undyed textiles—leathers, cottons,

A Painter By Providence

Fashion Sketches by Dee Beard Dean, 1987

silks and gauze—would then be dyed to her specifications to give an original and coordinated look to her mix-and-match pieces.

From her trips to Paris to attend the Prêt-à-Porter, the major international fashion exposition, Dee would return to Florida with inspirations for her collection (and a head start on the latest trends for the next season's color palette). The popularity of her line was partly based on Dee's choice of distinctive and evocative colors for her line, such as eggplant, sage, burnt sienna, turquoise and buttercream.

The Dee Beard Collections captured the look of romantic and multicultural influences. "My clothing was artsy with sculpted, breezy lines that flattered any figure," relates Dee. "Women would frequently tell me how they loved the unique look and comfortable feel of my pieces. I designed my clothing line to appeal to adventurous

people with a strong flair for fashion." Dee's fashions made bold and expressive statements that invited people to think and dream beyond the ordinary.

One of her favorite commercial design endeavors was her "New American" retail store and clothing label. The store was utterly unique at the time with its hip ambience sporting a yellow Cessna 150 airplane hanging from the ceiling. The store had an airport hanger look and shelves stacked with precisely folded clothing items. It was a fun-loving atmosphere and a unique shopping experience. In those days, it was not unusual to see locals or tourists strolling the sidewalks of Ft. Myers and Naples with Dee's "New American" logo emblazoned on their shirt or jeans.

Dee Beard Dean

Café Girl
oil on canvas
14 x 11 inches

All this commercial success led to an invitation to host fashion segments for a lifestyle TV program on a local station in Ft. Myers. With her TV appearances and hosting of runway shows at upscale malls in southwestern Florida, Dee became regarded as the area's foremost fashion expert.

The experience of designing, manufacturing and selling women's clothing gave Dee a head for business, yet she always managed to keep her hand in fine art. After a business associate took over the business, Dee began to relax her schedule and focus her expertise as a freelance designer for other clothing manufacturers. During her down time, Dee continued to paint landscapes and portraits, which was a welcome antidote to the fast and furious pace of the fashion industry.

Recalling those years, Dee speaks with gratitude about how she loved the glamour and hectic creativity of the fashion industry and how this business experience prior to becoming a full-time painter was truly a blessing. "It gave me the marketing know-how and structured self-discipline I needed to transition into the fine art world," comments Dee. "Most importantly, it gave me the diligence to get my work done everyday." In her painting workshops, she often sees how a lack of self-discipline in work habits seems to be the greatest obstacle to aspiring artists, many of whom are remarkably talented.

Dee has found that good business habits, such as regular working hours, negotiating skills, and accounting know-how, are all necessary in the art world as well. "Artists tend to be right-brained and creative at the expense of developing savvy business and marketing skills. It's easy to get stuck in one spot thinking talent alone is all you need, but to be a successful professional artist, left-brained skills are necessary as well," notes Dee.

Of course, the greatest underlying factor for success in art—as in any business—is motivation. Dee adds that, "Being an artist is not an easy profession. One must have a strong motivation to constantly observe, learn and improve through practice. It can be hard work and it can get discouraging, but successful artists just keep painting, knowing that no painting endeavor is ever a failure because you learn something from every canvas."

With a belief that every failure is but a step up toward greater knowledge and experience along the path to artistic recognition, Dee lives her life and career to the fullest potential, grasping opportunities and reaching for goals that most people would find too daunting.

The glamour, creativity and commercial success Dee enjoyed as a fashion designer was deeply satisfying, but after a whirlwind decade, fine art again moved to the top of her list of life ambitions. When the opportunity finally presented itself to become a full-time artist, Dee was ready and eager for the new challenge.

A Painter By Providence

Dee Beard Dean

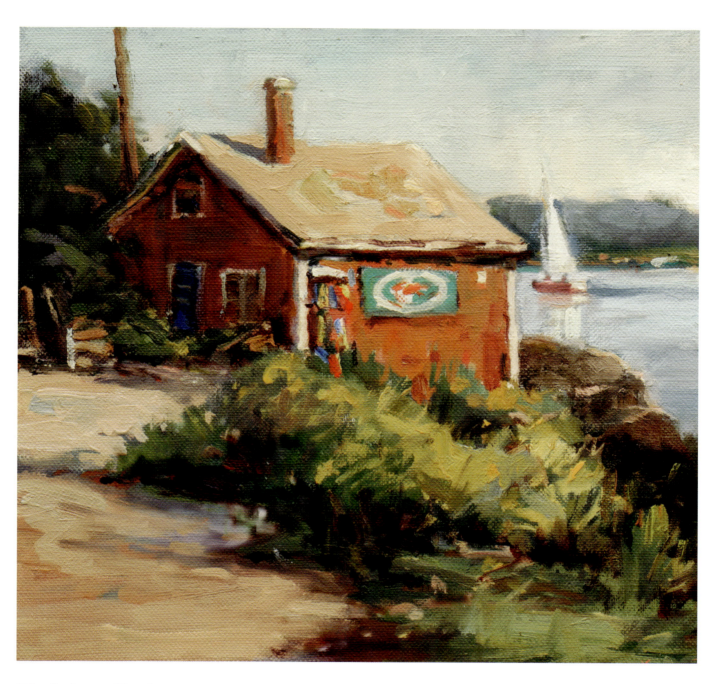

The Lobster Shack
oil on canvas
11 x 14 inches

A Painter By Providence

Mission Light
oil on canvas
16 x 20 inches

DEE BEARD DEAN

Lighthouse Blues
oil on canvas
12 x 12 inches

the substance of soul

In 1989, a business associate in the fashion industry who was familiar with Dee's fine art skills approached her about a project seeking works of original art. Real estate developers of a newly constructed resort condominium in North Carolina were looking for an artist to paint original oil landscapes for the interiors, and Dee's friend urged her to submit her portfolio for consideration. Many other artists had already sent in their portfolios in hopes of winning the commission, but Dee was the artist the builders selected to paint over 200 original oil paintings for the condos.

It was one of those defining moments which successful artists often describe, when the possibility of making a career transition into full-time painting seemed suddenly real. Dee spent the next several months composing and painting the 200 landscape works. She framed each one and delivered the lot to her patrons who were thrilled with the results. "It was grueling work creating and framing so many paintings at once. Yet, the opportunity taught me that painting was my true passion and lifelong desire. It was something I could do professionally and maintain a good income. I decided to phase out my clothing design career and began to paint every day instead," recalls Dee.

Her next lucky break came after she moved to Atlanta. Dee was offered studio space in the Galleria Specialty Mall in Atlanta during the Christmas season to paint pastel portraits while holiday shoppers strolled by. It was a temporary studio space designed to promote a festive ambience in the mall. Her work proved so appealing to shoppers, however, that the mall authorities asked Dee to stay and offered her the space as a permanent studio. After three years of painting in her mall studio, and with active participation in the Atlanta Portrait Society, Dee had a backlog of 40 portrait commissions and a growing national reputation.

Her acclaim as a portrait painter stems from her belief that everyone's inner character is echoed in their outward appearance. Portrait painting is not merely duplicating the look of a subject through observation, but rather creating a unified likeness where the outside persona radiates the subject's true personality with its eclectic mix of likes, dislikes, passions and peeves. Capturing the heart and soul of her subjects, Dee believes, requires getting to know their unique blend of persona and personality. This deeper understanding is something which confers character, substance and soul to the body's form.

Dee's philosophy and methods as a portrait artist involved first spending time with a subject, especially a child, in order to fully understand and know the person she was about to paint. This belief was validated through an experience with one commission involving painting two portraits at once—a deceased husband and wife, both of whom had been board members of a university.

Dee had only small photographs from which to paint their portraits, yet, she recalls, "Their son sat and talked with me for days while I painted and told me interesting stories and vignettes about his mother and father's life. He would offer suggestions about their physical features, which were not evident in the photographs. I was struck by how his anecdotes and insights helped me capture the likeness of two people whom I had never seen in person." The portraits were very well received, convincing her that knowledge of a subject's life experiences and personality can be encoded into the likeness of every subject.

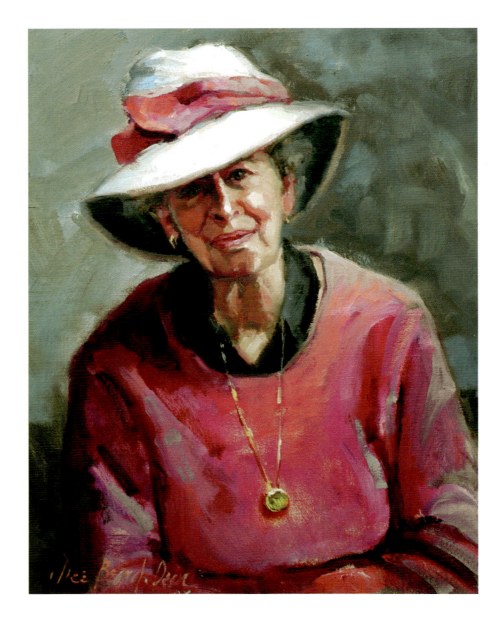

Portrait Sketch
Workshop Demonstration
oil on canvas
20 x 16 inches

Dee Beard Dean

Amber
oil on canvas
24 x 36 inches

Dee goes on to explain, "Whenever I now paint a portrait, I try to discover what is the indelible essence of my subject's personality. It's important, first of all, in composing the picture. You wouldn't want to pose an athletic boy, who is in his element on a football field, in formal attire sitting on a classic sofa. When I'm familiar with the thoughts and emotions of the person I'm painting, then I can paint intuitively as well as visually."

A portrait is a substantial financial investment for the patron so Dee assumes the responsibility of investing her time to observe and establish rapport with the subject. This relationship with the sitter is so important, in fact, that earlier in the history of this genre, portrait artists would often be invited to live with the patron's family for a while in order to get to know their subject firsthand.

DEE BEARD DEAN

Friends
oil on canvas
24 x 30 inches

Yellow Hats
(TOP LEFT)
oil on canvas
20 x 24 inches

Age of Wonder
(TOP RIGHT)
oil on canvas
20 x 24 inches

Through the years, Dee has discovered that a well-painted portrait, borne of a union between physical form and artistic interpretation, comes alive with meaning for the patron. "I often get the comment that a portrait's eyes follow the viewer, or that a viewer sees something new every day in a beloved portrait," observes Dee. "More so than with photographs, an image rendered by an artist's hand turns a portrait into a living memory undiminished by time."

Portuguese School-children
(BELOW)
oil on canvas
20 x 24 inches

Patrons become quite attached to a portrait of a family member, frequently telling her that, in case of a fire, after securing everyone's safety, the portrait is the first possession they would attempt to save. Children also tend to treasure their portraits as they grow older causing some parents, who had commissioned a portrait of the family, to wish they had painted their children separately so that each could inherit his or her own portrait.

Portrait commissions often turn into deeply touching and moving experiences for Dee. She recalls a young man she painted posthumously who had died from AIDS and another whom she had to paint from video clips taken prior to the young man's suicide. In both cases, the mothers wept with overpowering sadness and joy at the sight of Dee's finished portraits.

Dee sees her talent as a way for God to bring both joy and healing to others. Portraits of loved ones, and even painted landscapes, can have a profound impact on viewers' emotions, reminding patrons of treasured people and places, or of defining events in their lives. Dee recalls a painting she made of a location in England, which she later posted on her website. A couple saw the painting online and sent an e-mail to Dee explaining that they had been in that exact spot on vacation and very much wished to purchase the painting.

A powerful subconscious connection exists between art, memory and emotion. Art can energize important memories which have lain dormant for years and animate them with renewed life and vitality. Hanging portrait and landscape works is a way to honor our loved ones and the places where we once enjoyed ourselves, adding a sense of mindfulness and serenity to our busy, overly-scheduled lives.

For the artist, the joy of painting a portrait doesn't end with the unveiling, but extends vicariously through the enduring satisfaction it bestows upon the viewers.

A Painter By Providence

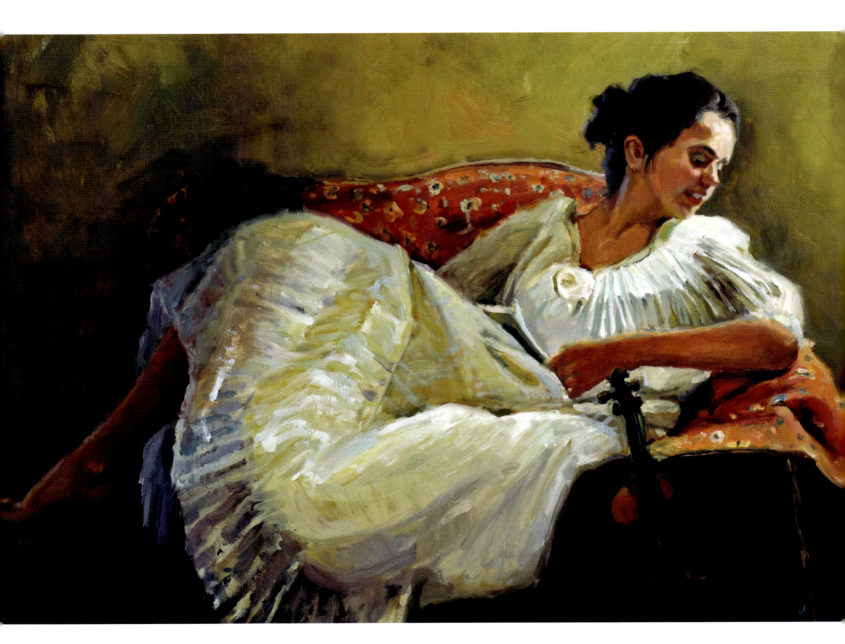

Repose
oil on canvas
24 x 36 inches

Dee Beard Dean

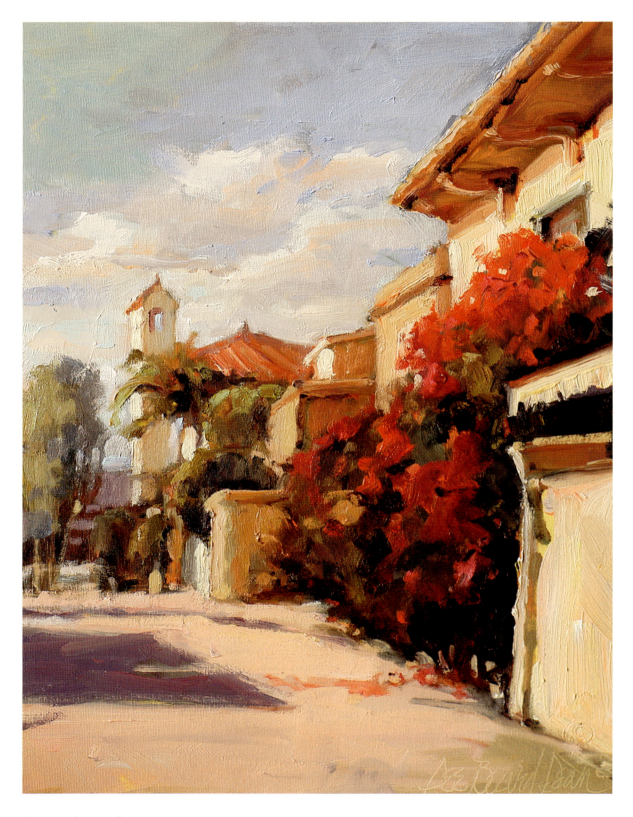

Spanish Azaleas
oil on canvas
20 x 16 inches

Dr. Nicolai
oil on canvas
24 x 20 inches

DEE BEARD DEAN

Poppy Fields
oil on canvas
20 x 24 inches

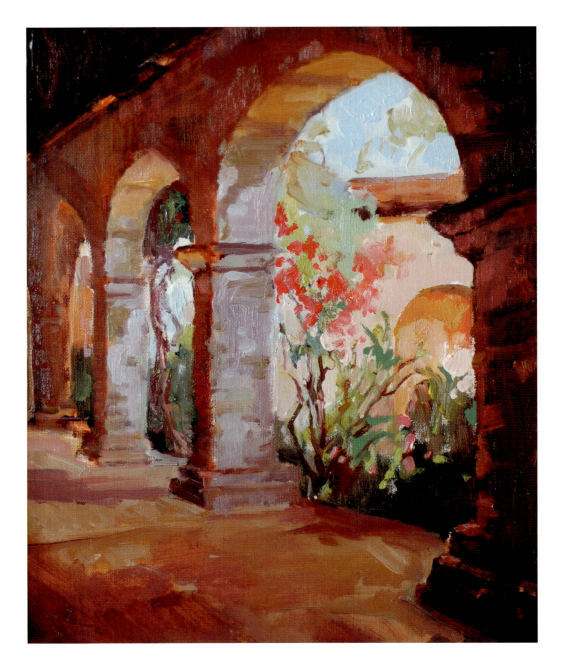

Sunlit Arches
oil on canvas
14 x 11 inches

Flower Pickers
oil on canvas
16 x 20 inches

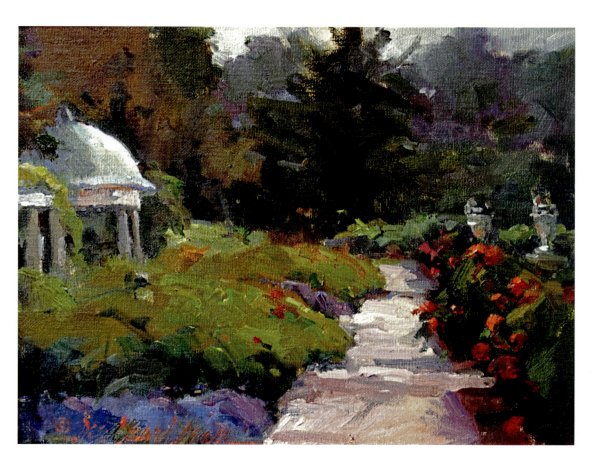

Italian Gardens
oil on canvas
11 x 14 inches

a kaleidoscope of colors

From painting portraiture, Dee had earned widespread and respected recognition for capturing the likeness, vitality and character of her sitters. Though the manner of her brushwork was loose and painterly, the facial peculiarities of her subjects—the contour of a cheekbone, the jut of the chin, or the light and shadow patterns falling upon the planes of a face—were painted true to life. With impressionistic brushstrokes, Dee imparted authentic realism and a feeling of solidity to the head and body.

While commissioned portraits fully occupied her painting schedule, Dee's love of the great outdoors began to lure her outside the studio. During a pivotal excursion one day painting with fellow artist, Gwen Nagel, a landscape artist from Athens, Georgia, Dee discovered how inspiring and invigorating it was to paint for hours under the open sky, *en plein air* (French for out-of-doors). Smitten by the ever-shifting shadows, light and color, Dee was hooked by the wonderful illusion of reality these spontaneous visual effects produced on canvas.

She found painting landscapes to be very liberating and creative, since achieving an exact likeness to the outdoor scene was not as critical as it is when painting the topography of a person's face. "In composing landscapes, you can choose to take out or leave in a tree to enhance the composition, but in portrait painting, you have no choice about putting in two eyes, a nose and mouth. Likewise, to paint a person's head, an artist is limited by distinct boundaries in defining the form," explains Dee. "In landscape painting, many of the forms are organic and not necessarily precise in shape, so the choices for problem solving, improvising and experimentation are endless. For instance, besides deciding what to leave in and edit out, a landscape artist must decide how to achieve a sense of depth or distance with aerial perspective, how to render the foreground, middle and background masses, and how to compose the four major planes of a scene. I enjoy the infinite challenges and choices of painting landscapes," she says.

While similarities exist in painting portraits and landscapes, such as the use of edges and color to push some objects back and pull others forward, the challenges specific to painting outdoors sharpened Dee's vision and skills beyond what she could have achieved in the studio. Her eyes became highly attuned to the movement and interplay of light and shadow, while her brushstrokes quickened and became more expressive with color and emotion. Immersing herself in the landscape genre soon endowed Dee with a new level of knowledge and repertoire of skills, which in turn, added a richer, more painterly dimension to her portrait works.

With her newfound passion for painting *en plein air* and for rendering nature's infinite displays of mood, atmosphere and color schemes on canvas, it was the Impressionists to whom Dee turned for further study and guidance. French Impressionism was a movement that began in the latter half of the nineteenth century and represented a shift in artistic mission and style from studio painting—with its layers

Cortona at Noon
oil on canvas
24 x 24 inches

DEE BEARD DEAN

Red Cliffs
oil on canvas
12 x 24 inches

John Wayne Haynes
oil on canvas
12 x 24 inches

Ready and Waiting
oil on canvas
16 x 20 inches

Dee Beard Dean

Progreso Beach Vendor
oil on canvas
24 x 24 inches

of glazed pigments applied over time—to the spontaneous, *alla prima* (all in one session) interpretations of the glorious colors and light of nature.

A technological breakthrough—the invention of paint tubes—was credited as a major factor in the evolution of this new artistic style. Paint tubes allowed artists greater freedom and mobility to travel outdoors in all types of weather and capture their immediate impressions of a locale. Painting out in the open, from dawn to dusk, the Impressionists chose mood and atmosphere to dominate the scene. They adopted a wide range of colors and textured brushstrokes that were as quick and lively as the shifting light effects.

In America, the Impressionist movement branched into a number of different "schools" and Dee was most struck by the teaching methods, and landscape/outdoor figure paintings of the Cape Cod School of Art. This school was a group of influential artists whose teachings on color theory captured Dee's inquisitive imagination. She was inspired by their abiding pursuit of creating luminosity through modulating warm and cool color temperatures.

Charles Webster Hawthorne in Provincetown, Massachusetts, founded the Cape Cod School of Art and leadership of the school was passed down to successive protégés dedicated to the School's traditional teachings. Dee rigorously read books and studied the lively paintings of the founders and their followers, most notably Charles Webster Hawthorn, Emile A. Gruppé and Henry Hensche.

The colorist movement in America, spawned in part by The Cape Cod School of Art tradition, has been passed down to many notable contemporary painters. Their works reveal dramatic compositions with innovative and color-laden brushstrokes that excite the senses and breathe life and dynamism into every scene. The simple, direct brushwork and vibrating colors, designed to convey the artist's emotional intrigue in a locale, represent the hallmarks of this tradition. In following the methods of this School, Dee developed an academic eye for painting luminous landscapes using subtle contrasts and harmonies of color—warm against cool, saturated against subdued, and light against dark.

Of the American Impressionists' works, Dee was most taken with the painterly compositions and teachings on color theory of a second-generation American painter, Emile A. Gruppé, who spent much of his childhood in the Netherlands, then moved back to the United States to live and paint the clear light and maritime scenery of New England. In reading Gruppé's books, Dee came to appreciate how the value and role of every hue in a painting does not exist in isolation, but rather reacts in a communal sense to the whole. This creates optical effects such that the behavior and appearance of each color is determined by the colors surrounding it. "Early on, I would apply lots of bright color to any scene. Then, of course, the painting became all about color," explained Dee. "I wanted my paintings to be more about the quality of light, and the truthfulness of how light describes a subject. Now, instead of covering every canvas with saturated colors, I realize that being faithful to the scene is all about understanding the proper relationship between warm and cool, and saturated and subdued colors. Just like human personalities, some colors are outgoing and some are shy. It's the combination and layering of these contrasts that build the visual excitement and beauty in a painting."

After years of painting from life and on location, Dee has toned down her use of bold colors and cultivated a deeper appreciation for more muted colors, both for the poetic, evocative radiance of soft grays, and also for their ability to act as foils for the brighter, more intense colors. Her works masterfully demonstrate how a canvas orchestrated with

Foggy Day in St. Andrews
oil on canvas
11 x 14 inches

muted colors can appear more powerful than a painting covered corner to corner with intense color—for what the grayed down colors lack in intensity, they more than make up for in visual impact when placed next to intense colors.

"The optical effect of a tonal color next to a bright color invariably makes the brighter color pop and appear much more eye-catching and rich than it would otherwise appear by itself or surrounded by equally bright colors. I love harmonious grays because they don't fight with the brighter colors and they give the painting a softer, more pleasing look and feel. I frequently recommend to my students to do studies where they might surround a colorful object, such as a colorful boat, with grayed colors, and watch how it makes the colors appear to pop out more than if they had painted it surrounded by other bright colors."

Dee Beard Dean

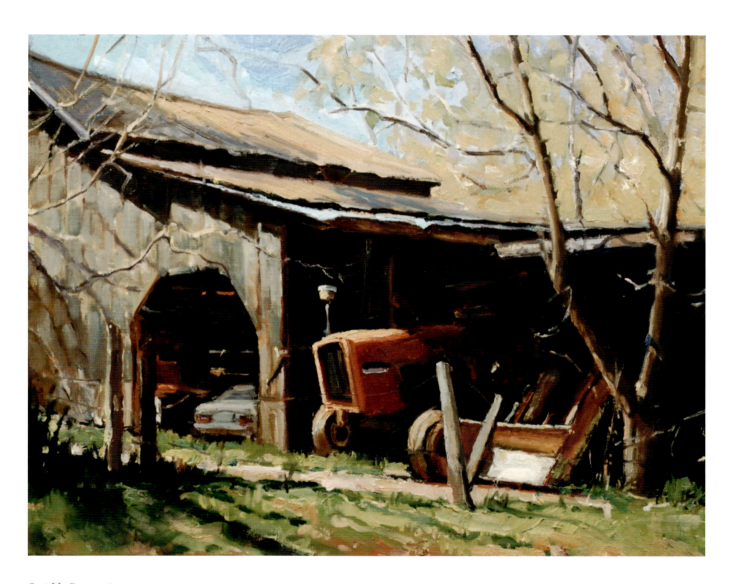

Still Running
oil on canvas
16 x 20 inches

Wave Dance
oil on canvas
11 x 14 inches

Dee Beard Dean

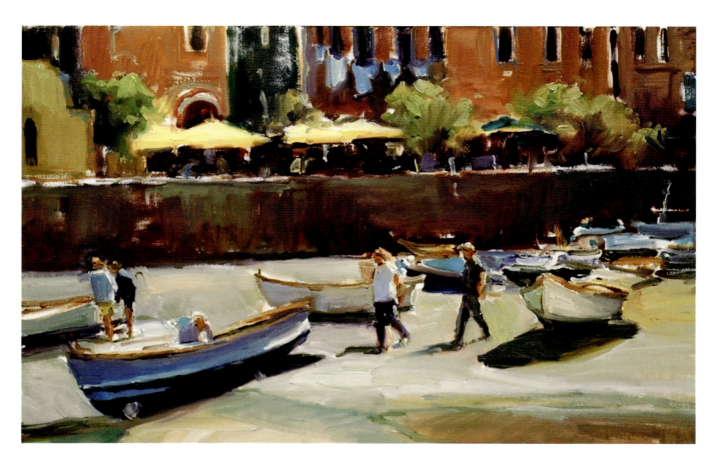

Launch Break
oil on canvas
16 x 20 inches

A Painter By Providence

Donatella's Villa
oil on canvas
30 x 24 inches

Dee Beard Dean

Where the Swallows Come (LEFT)
oil on canvas
24 x 24 inches

Dee shares with other Impressionists a joyous obsession with shimmering color, yet she does not describe herself as a colorist but rather as an Impressionistic Realist. She sees the essential beauty of a subject in terms of how light reveals a subject's color relationships. Her goal in painting landscapes or portraits is to capture a striking harmonious glow—or luminosity—on canvas with accurate tonal values and contrasting warm and cool color temperatures.

In her own works, she strives to achieve colors that are emphasized and strengthened, but not exaggerated to the point of making them appear unrealistic. As such, her paintings are not defined by a signature color palette, so much as a feeling of authenticity imbued with the painter's own devout love for the beauty and brevity of the outdoor moment.

Dee allows each scene to dictate the color scheme, whether dominated by soft grays—like that of a cloud-covered salt marsh—or overflowing with bold, riotous hues—like that of a Mexican courtyard. This flexibility in palette creates believable landscapes that offer the eye a dreamy visual escape into a locale where highlights sparkle and shadows are washed in mystery.

Dee Beard Dean

Mountain Shadows Study
oil on canvas
11 x 14 inches

A Painter By Providence

Tall Coastal Pines
oil on canvas
30 x 24 inches

Corchie Italian Retreat
oil on canvas
30 x 30 inches

seeing the splendor

By the early 1990s, Dee's popularity as a landscape artist increasingly brought invitations to teach painting workshops throughout the Southeast. Her teaching methods—based on the methodology and color theories of the Cape Cod School of Art—focused on color relationships, and in teaching this method, Dee quickly advanced the skills of her workshop students. Says Dee, "I always begin my workshops with lessons in color theory which I find helps the students maximize their progress. Some artists I teach often do not have a thorough understanding of color theory, while others simply were taught incorrect information. Making the colors in a painting 'sing' can only happen with proper or intuitive mixing of the colors on the palette and also on the canvas. Using color contrasts effectively is typically an advanced skill, but can be acquired more rapidly through understanding."

Dee has found that, as beginners, artists tend to paint with primary colors straight out of the tube. As they gain experience and a little knowledge of color theory, however, their tastes change to reflect a more complex understanding of color harmony and the ways subtle contrasts in temperature and intensity can enhance

Dee Beard Dean

Burning Off
oil on canvas
11 x 14 inches

the beauty of any scene or object. Whenever students grasp this understanding of contrasts, it becomes an epiphany that can propel them to a higher level.

In her workshops, Dee first tries to strengthen her students' understanding of color relationships, knowing that greater technique and execution soon follow. "I teach students not what color "formula" to use, but what color to use to achieve a proper relationship," she says. "This way they can interpret any subject in their own unique way, rather than merely duplicate an object's exact color and form.

Dee teaches that creating pleasing, beautiful artwork is ultimately about having good taste in both color harmony and composition. She relates how, in choosing a subject and composition, students often spend too much time in the field or studio searching for striking or dramatically beautiful scenes to paint. Says Dee, "I offer my students a quote by Charles Hawthorne which reads, 'anything under the sun is beautiful if you have the vision—it is the seeing of the thing that makes it so.' This ability to see the beauty of light itself and its relationship to the form is what I try to ingrain in my students rather than focus on duplicating the form."

When art students begin to see the hidden or unnoticed beauty in mundane surroundings, then a taste for simplicity in design, sophisticated color relationships and sure intention begins to materialize on their canvases, often in a matter of days. Dee can tell students have made this leap in understanding when they quit searching vigilantly for grandiose subjects to paint. With more discerning eyes, they begin to choose compositions painted with fewer brushstrokes yet rich with nuances in color and light, emphasizing the extraordinary play of light falling on a simple object, an unusual juxtaposition in color harmony or tonal value, or the curious tinges of color in a bright white object or a dark shadow.

Once an artist acquires this visual acuity and heightened awareness of light effects, the world can appear much richer and luminescent than it once did. Dee relates that "I see beauty in absolutely everything, sometimes to my detriment because anywhere I go, I'm surrounded by countless focal points begging to be painted."

Dee remembers learning this lesson herself during a *plein air* painting workshop she took years ago with renowned instructor and landscape painter George Strickland. As the class walked through a parking lot, George stopped in his tracks when a strong reflection of light bouncing off a Volkswagen caught his eye. Instead of painting a nearby landscape to demonstrate for the class, he set up his easel right there in the parking lot and painted the light hitting that car.

"To me, as long as you have light, you have beauty," muses Dee. "It doesn't take a European street scene or an awe-inspiring mountain vista to produce a painting with luminous light. Any simple, everyday scene such as rays of morning sun streaming through a kitchen window, or a cast shadow on the side of a building, can be rendered in stunning light and color."

In addition to teaching the fundamentals of art, Dee also imparts in her students an enthusiasm for painting every subject under the sun. "Versatility is one of my strengths and it happened because I never wanted to specialize in any one area," says Dee. "I love it all—all color combinations on the palette, all subjects and mediums, and sculpting as well as painting. Even the clothing lines I designed were just another medium with which to express my love of creating art through color, design and texture."

Her reverie for the infinite displays of beauty and her eye for absorbing obscure details are deeply rooted in her daily outdoor experiences during childhood. As a young girl, the quiescent beauty of the family farms and forested plains of Indiana

A Painter By Providence

Day's Work Done
oil on canvas
11 x 14 inches

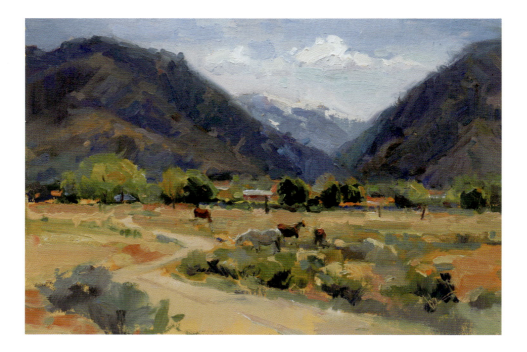

Springtime in Arroyo Seco
oil on canvas
11 x 14 inches

often occupied Dee's thoughts as she hiked through open fields, watched rabbits feed in the soft morning light, or played with neighborhood friends on a summer evening. "Life was slower and more reflective and I had so much beauty to look at and wonder about. These days, I worry about kids spending lots of time indoors engaged in electronic games in which the lessons are cyber-based and otherworldly. These games leave little in the way of inspiration or real world experience and they keep children from being drawn in by the beauty of life that surrounds them. Developing an artistic mind doesn't happen automatically, but rather must be nurtured through years of observation, inspiration, experience and education," notes Dee.

Artists are the true students of life. They need to continually hone their observation skills, develop a reflective outlook, practice their craft and hunger for more knowledge of the world around them in order to heighten their sensitivities and see all the artistic possibilities. "I used to think of art as a talent someone is born with, but most of the time, artists are not born, they are created," comments Dee. "To become accomplished, artists have to go through miles and miles of study, observation and practice." In his seminal book *The Art Spirit*, Robert Henri writes, "To apprehend beauty is to work for it."

For every artist, a challenge to the learning process is mastering the balancing act between knowledge and skill. "I find that if students take too many workshops in a short time, this can confuse an aspiring artist more than help him or her. A student should take a workshop, and then spend time putting into practice what was learned. One can only grasp so much in a class, and may not understand everything at once. But with practice, whatever knowledge was gleaned from an instructor will begin to make sense. When an artist feels ready for the next challenge, he or she should take another workshop to advance to the next level," advises Dee.

The artistic journey, Dee feels, is a back and forth process between studying the fundamentals and practicing the skills. Hence, the learning curve for an art student looks less like a curve and more like a stair step where progress is made one step at a time.

Students also progress quickly in Dee's workshops in part because she wastes no effort altering a person's innate style in color sense or brushwork. Dee believes it's important to honor each artist's unique way of self-expression and to simply share with students the intellectual tools needed to make the most of their creative abilities. "I learned while painting side-by-side with my son, John, that two artists can see the same object, yet render it on canvas in very different colors and brushstrokes. Since everyone sees differently, my objective is not to make students see or paint like I do. Only to understand the universal principles that will make any color scheme or composition look better," Dee emphasizes. "With the freedom to express and interpret subjects in their own style, artists acquire greater confidence and feel less frustration in pushing their own limits."

Encouragement, Dee believes, is something as vital to aspiring artists as is study and practice. Dee recalls a particular incident as a youngster when she was drawing on her front porch one day while a group of children were in the yard playing softball. A neighbor woman came over to watch Dee draw and commented, "Those other kids out there are having a good time, but you're doing something that will help you for the rest of your life. You're very good at this! You should keep on doing it."

Words of encouragement such as this can elevate self-esteem and boost a person's courage to take risks. Conversely, a few words of discouragement can destroy the drive to be creative. Because of her deep gratitude for all the encouragement she received as a child, Dee cautions people to "be careful what you say to your children and grandchildren who show a creative side to their personalities. It will remain with them forever, for better or worse. And if it gets destroyed, then with what will they fill the creative void in their life that will provide the same level of satisfaction?"

From her own experiences, she knows that art can benefit all aspects of a person's life: Creating art satisfies the desire for achievement; it can offer immediate gratification and emotional healing; and it can fulfill a creative void or lack of purpose in a person's life.

Orosi Valley
oil on canvas
30 x 30 inches

Two Boats
oil on canvas
12 x 20 inches

"Often, artists tend to have a strong sense of mission about making art their life's work. This can be both a blessing and a curse because if one has it, the desire cannot be suppressed. The best thing to do is simply pick up a paintbrush and enjoy the satisfaction of creating art," Dee says with a smile. "Art feeds the artistic soul like food for the psyche. It simply nourishes the creative spirit."

Art has always supplied Dee with the inner strength to continue pursuing her dreams. Yet, in her workshops and through interacting with so many aspiring art students over the years, she sees how frequently people struggle with all the distractions in life that keep them from pursuing their creative ambitions. Too often, people have worrisome obstacles to overcome and sometimes a crippling fear of failure, all of which can destroy their intentions to paint. She advises her students that the

Squash Pot
oil on canvas
30 x 24 inches

most difficult part of painting is getting to the studio. She, herself, admits to having struggled for many years with "art demons" that threw every possible distraction in her path to keep her from her easel. Unstoppable determination is what artists need to keep painting despite the distractions and the discouragements that seem to perpetually afflict creative souls.

In time, however, the struggle and frustration gives way to a restless eagerness to paint something every day. "It's a strange phenomenon how artists start out with such reluctance to paint, then later feel anxious if they miss so much as a day in the studio," remarks Dee. Though her compulsion to paint has always been a source of joy and healing in her life, Dee doesn't feel that the satisfaction she derives from painting is her true driving force. Rather, she recognized at a very early age she had a special gift for creative self-expression through art, which, in her adult years, grew into a spiritual mission and responsibility to develop her talents to the fullest extent.

Through her workshops and studio classes, Dee realized she also had a gift for teaching art, specifically in helping students understand color theory. With a knack for explaining complicated principles in simple, easy-to-grasp concepts, and for demonstrating how proper color relationships can energize a canvas, Dee enjoys the artistic growth this knowledge produces in her students. "Teaching art also speeds the learning process for the instructor. I always encourage other skilled artists to teach workshops because the more I teach, the more I learn. Teaching continually reinforces, reconfirms and clarifies the principles of landscape painting in my own mind," explains Dee.

Sunlit Cottage
oil on canvas
11 x 14 inches

Throughout her art career, she has helped men and women of all ages find their gifts and fulfill their creative drive. Many of Dee's family members including her sister, daughter and son are professional artists, and she has taught workshops to countless students, some of whom have become successful gallery artists. Passing on a legacy of creative learning, artistic excellence and encouragement is what she now finds most invigorating in her professional career.

Today, whether creating her own fine art or teaching painting in her workshops, Dee always keeps the bar high, sharing whatever dose of know-how, encouragement and persistence necessary to meet the challenge.

Dee Beard Dean

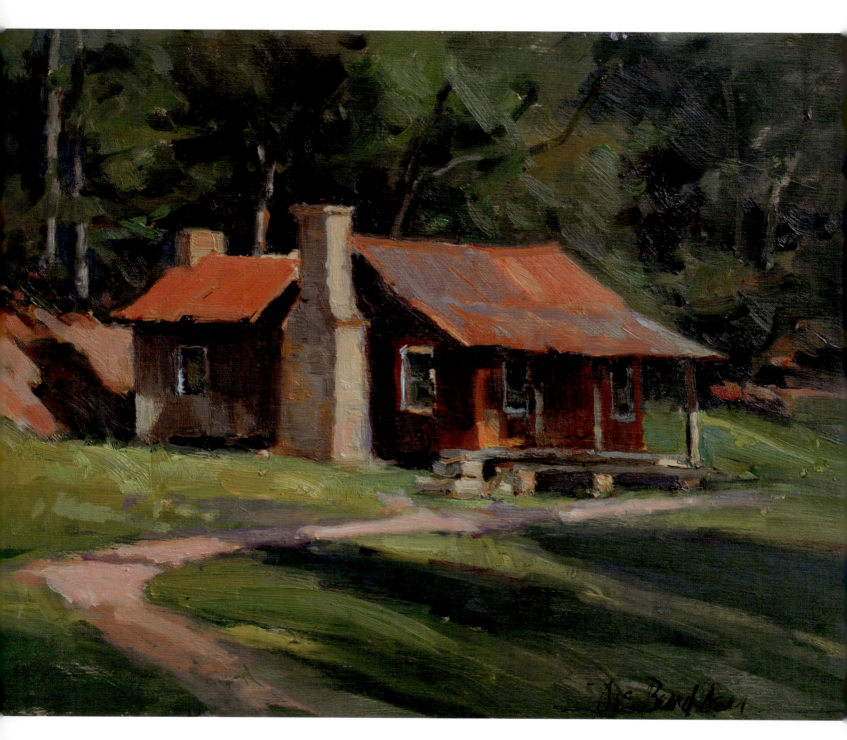

Keyes Cabin
oil on canvas
11 x 14 inches

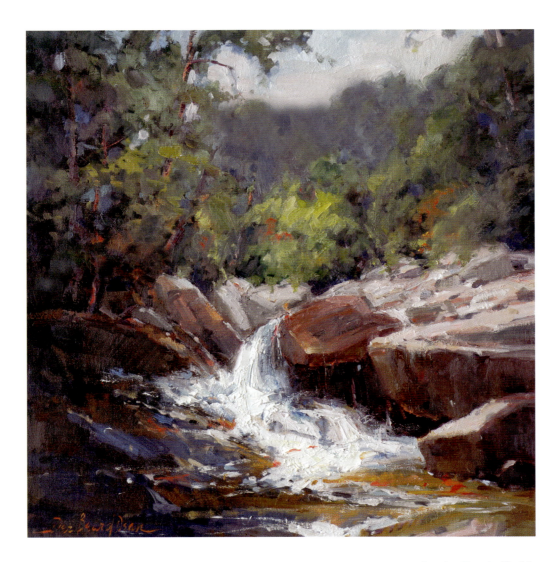

Joe's Fork Falls
oil on canvas
24 x 24 inches

Dee Beard Dean

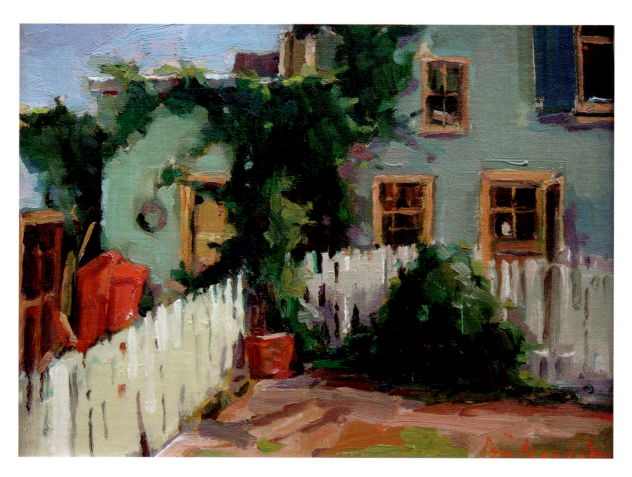

Backyard Antiques
oil on canvas
16 x 20 inches

A Painter By Providence

Chateaux and Vineyard
oil on canvas
24 x 30 inches

Dee Beard Dean

the beauty of plein air painting

In *plein air* painting, the brushwork is truly the poetry of the painting. Rich in texture, color, meaning, and layers of emotions such as joy and confidence, brushstokes reveal the artist's innermost feelings at the moment the pigment was applied to the canvas.

Because atmospheric light changes so quickly, altering all the pattern shapes of light and shadow in a scene, *plein air* painters must learn to economize their decision-making, their palette colors and their rendering of details. This process creates small paintings that are spontaneous, fresh and rarely cluttered or overworked. Painting quickly, a single broad brushstroke might signify a field of flowers or the entire sky.

This method teaches painters how to hone in on the most important issues of composition and focal point, and how to create alluring contrasts using values or temperature.

Since a painter's brushwork is his or her authentic signature, it's good to spend time painting under the sun, and let nature teach the basics about how to make the greatest impact with the least expense of time and brushwork.

Artists are blessed because we never have a dull moment. As visual creatures, we live in a world full of excitement and joy drawn from the simple ability to see beyond the ordinary.

—Dee Beard Dean

Photo by Nick Chalfa

From years of experience as an outdoor painter, Dee's creative inspiration and skills have quickened to capture eye-catching images with vigorous accuracy and spontaneity. In these images, Dee is painting in a Cowboy Quick Draw competition organized by the Plein Air Painters of the Southeast (PAP-SE) in August 2009, at Leatherwood Mountains in North Carolina. For this event, PAP-SE invited outdoor painters and painting groups from around the Southeast to gather for an Outdoor Painter's Forum that included workshops and group paint-outs amidst the

"Hugh" Plein Air
oil on canvas
12 x 16 inches

glorious Blue Ridge mountain scenery.

Paint outs such as this one challenge a painter's art-making skills to keep the painting stylistically fresh and better convey the immediate impact of the subject. Additionally, one must maintain accuracy in color harmony, draftsmanship and tonal value despite the changing sunlight and limited time frame in which to create the work of art. Audiences watching the artists demonstrate their *plein air* skills invariably come away with a greater appreciation and understanding of the ever-fascinating creative process.

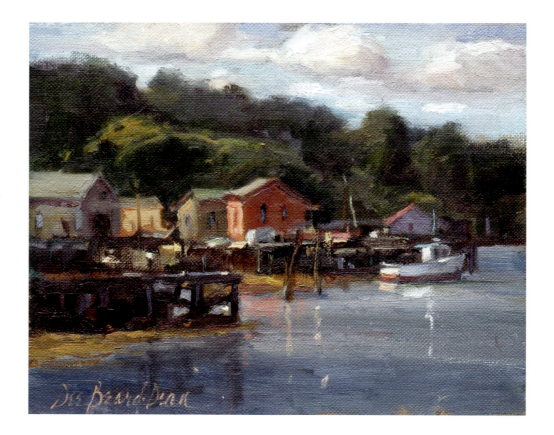

The Last Light of Day
oil on canvas
9 x 12 inches

Market Shopping
oil on canvas
11 x 14 inches

A PAINTER BY PROVIDENCE

studies and quick sketches

Athens Clock
oil on canvas
10 x 8 inches

Charleston Tour
oil on canvas
11 x 14 inches

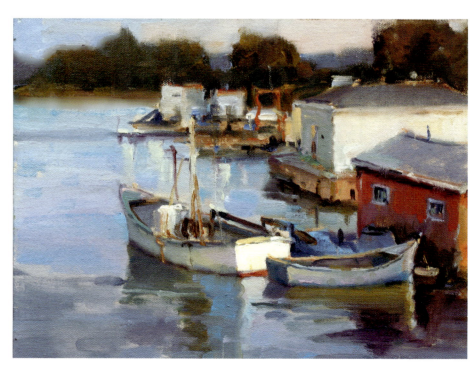

Little Red Boathouse
oil on canvas
11 x 14 inches

On Distant Mountain
oil on canvas
16 x 20 inches

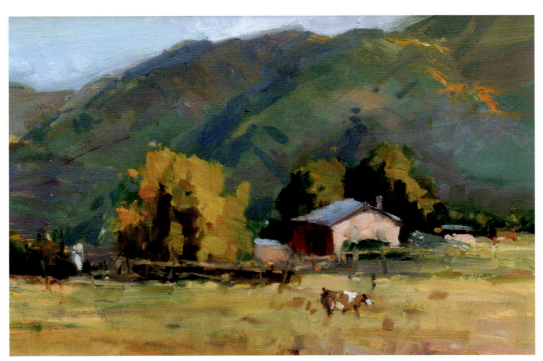

Aspen Country
oil on canvas
16 x 20 inches

Tall Palms
oil on canvas
20 x 20 inches

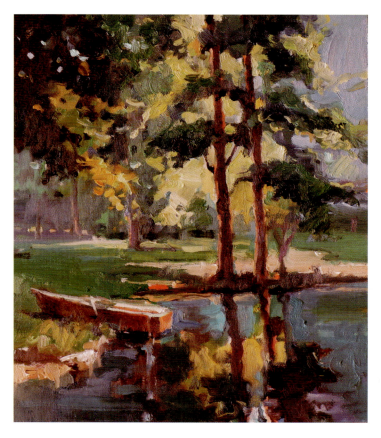

Red Boat
oil on canvas
14 x 11 inches

Beaver Creek Canoes
oil on canvas
6 x 8 inches

Mallards
oil on canvas
11 x 14 inches

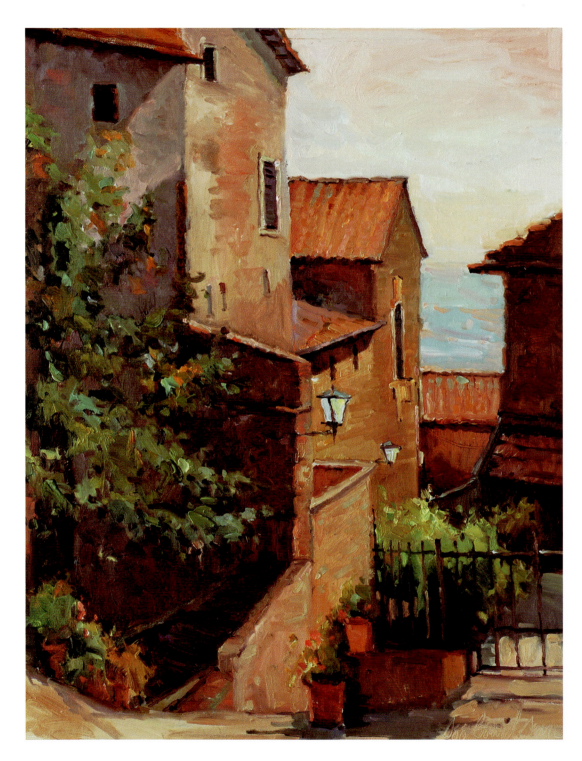

A Small View
oil on canvas
30 x 24 inches

Ancient One
oil on canvas
20 x 16 inches

DEE BEARD DEAN

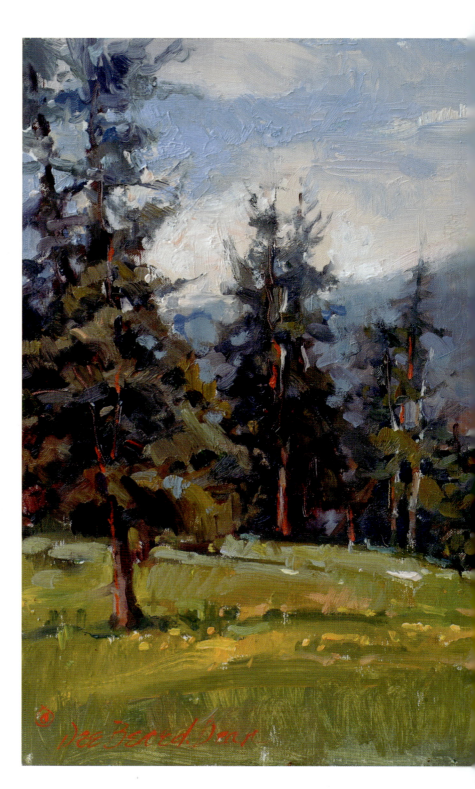

New Mexico Dandelions
oil on canvas
16 x 20 inches

Dee Beard Dean

Maria, the Navajo Girl
oil on canvas
20 x 16 inches

the allure of light

Light is to an open-air painter what energy is to a scientist: A mesmerizing and ever-mysterious phenomenon. Since childhood, Dee has been infinitely curious about visual manifestations of light—how sunlight undulates on the water's surface, how it describes an object's shape, color and texture, and how it permeates the air above a desert, ocean, mountain or pasture with mood. Adding to the beauty and mystery of it all is how the appearance and play of light changes with every passing moment. The sun, in its journey from horizon to horizon, sheds a multi-colored spectrum, transforming the brightness and scheme of colors continuously as it arcs across the sky.

"It's so awe-inspiring to see the luminosity of everyday objects and scenery. It gives me a sense of connection to God who created all this phenomenal beauty," says Dee. "My heightened awareness of light and its visual qualities makes the world so intriguing. Because of this, I enjoy every day, whether gray and cloudy, or bright and sunny. With the eyes of an artist, each day and location presents me with a completely new and different impression."

This all-consuming love of atmospheric light has coaxed Dee to many exotic countries around the world. In foreign lands, the beguiling light and ancient cultures—each with their unique and colorful traditions—offer exciting compositional possibilities from nearly every street corner.

For an artist in love with light, color, culture and geography, travel and painting go hand in hand. The novelty of new lands while intermingling with diverse peoples elevates the senses, causing artists to feel intensely alive and awestruck. Like a muse that summons the rarified emotions, travel has always invigorated Dee's creativity. She loves to render the vibrant styles of local costumes or fashion, the rustic textures of fabrics, the tangy smells of unfamiliar fruits and vegetables sold in street markets, and the drama of timeworn architecture and landscapes. As Harvard philosopher George Santayana puts it: travel "sharpens the edges of life."

Today, Dee travels several times a year to different countries to paint the scenery and to conduct painting workshops. "I enjoy teaching workshops in other countries because as spectators to the new sights, topography, people and food, my students feel a surge of emotion-charged energy. A landscape painting is really an emotional record of a place," comments Dee, and travel simply enhances the emotional appeal to any environment, especially if experiencing it for the first time.

She especially enjoys introducing her students to the diversity of new cultures such as in San Miguel, Mexico where Dee fell in love with the charming sights and sounds of the Mexican people: the playful children, the traditional costumes, the community camaraderie. Recalls Dee, "I realize now how my clothing designs and the European labels I sold in my stores were really about promoting an appreciation for human diversity and distinctive cultures. My clothing appealed to the type of men and women who radiated a confident, artsy and adventurous spirit—the kind of people who love to travel around the world as I do."

From her own trips to Ecuador, Mexico, Italy, France, Greece, Costa Rica and Spain, Dee has gained an even deeper appreciation of how clothing is about more

Yemeni Man
oil on canvas
11 x 14 inches

Dee Beard Dean

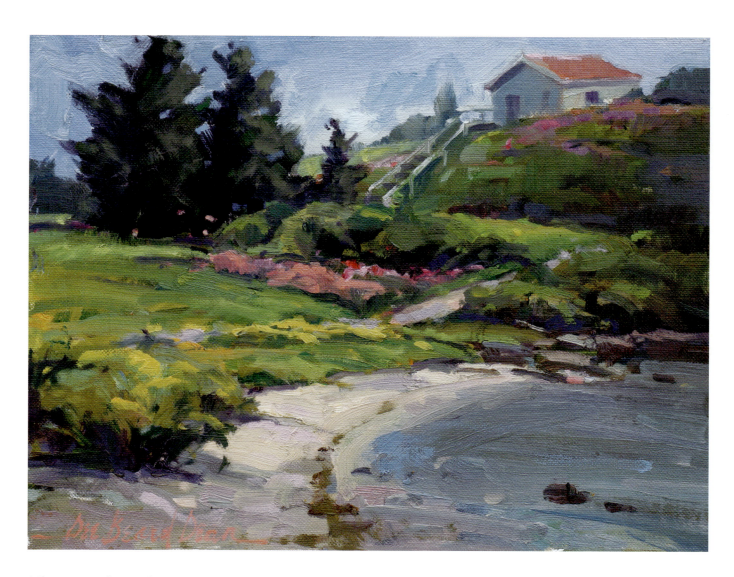

The Bay of Fundy
oil on canvas
11 x 14 inches

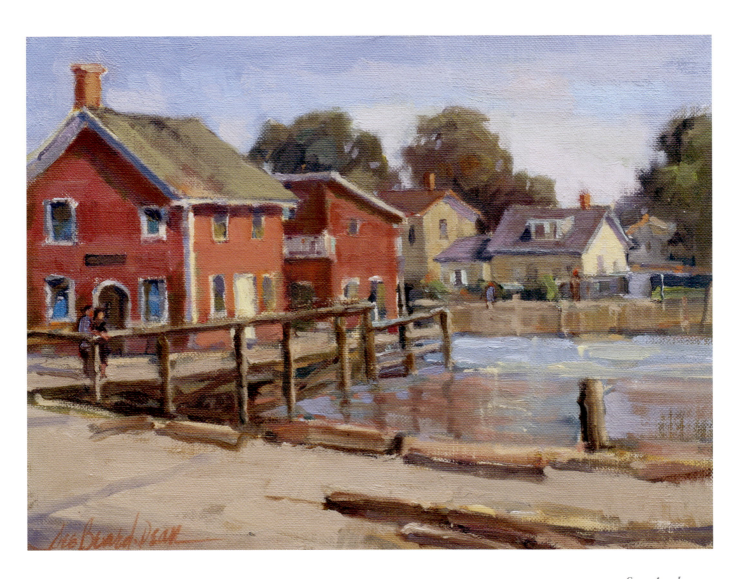

St. Andrews
oil on canvas
11 x 14 inches

Dee Beard Dean

Morning at Arroyo Seco Church
oil on canvas
12 x 12 inches

Old Vineyard
oil on canvas
11 x 14 inches

than just fun or fashion. A distinctive manner of dress gives people a secure sense of identity and belonging, whether to a city, rural community, tribe or family. Clothing, jewelry and hairstyles worn in particular ways can advertise very personal information such as class, profession, personality or marital status. Typically, the traditional fashion of a region tells many stories about its people and their history, which is why well-traveled artists love to interpret on canvas the multi-hued cultures they witness in their expeditions around the globe.

So much of human history is founded upon the insatiable curiosity of intrepid souls who ventured outside their conventional roles or native lands to seek new discoveries. From the earliest cave drawings, art is often the medium by which knowledge of the world, at large, is transmitted. Dee has always viewed art as a satisfying way of communicating one person's experience of life with others. It provides her with a spiritual connection to the world and a way to magnify its wonders.

Dee remembers how a newspaper reporter in Athens, Georgia, where she once lived, wrote a story about her painting trip to Portugal, then sent the article to the editor of her hometown newspaper, the La Grange News. To her great surprise, Dee received many wonderful letters and e-mails from people with whom she grew up saying, "I always wondered what you did with your artwork!" One letter came from her high school principal, who wrote a heartwarming letter in response to the article. Dee has found, time and again, that art brings people together through a mutual love for adventure travel and authentic living.

Dee also travels frequently around the United States to participate in juried shows and other major art events, most of which occur in the West. She began to realize that, though the Southeast was brimming with great Southern artists,

A Painter By Providence

New Mexico Summer
oil on canvas
16 x 20 inches

The Little Homestead
oil on canvas
16 x 20 inches

141

Dee Beard Dean

Windswept Beach
oil on canvas
16 x 20 inches

her region of the country was hardly represented in the shows and gatherings of prestigious national arts organizations. And though she loved networking with other notable artists in the west coast shows, Dee also yearned for the companionship of fellow professional artists closer to home. Painting together in beautiful locales is a satisfying experience for artists, as is sharing ideas, news and methods about the art world. "Painting in the studio is very solitary," admits Dee. "A full-time artist needs to get out of the studio and spend time with other creative people."

After one trip to the annual art exhibition by the Plein Air Painters of America (PAPA) at Laguna Beach, California, Dee decided to do more to encourage camaraderie among professional artists in her region and to attract art collectors to Southeastern galleries and art shows. She followed the advice of acclaimed landscape painter George Strickland to build a professional organization of *plein air* painters living and working in the Southeast.

Consequently, in 2001 Dee founded—along with a few other founding members—the Plein Air Painters of the Southeast. The mission of this core group of painters was threefold: to hone their painting skills through the demanding rigors of painting outdoors; to enjoy the camaraderie and shared knowledge of fellow *plein air* painters; and, to raise awareness and appreciation of the traditional method of painting *en plein air* among art connoisseurs and collectors.

To ensure a high level of professionalism and expertise, Dee and her colleagues decided to add only a few new members every year through a juried process. In selecting the new members, the group looked at an applicant's academic training and reputation, but outstanding talent was the main criterion. Says Dee, "Looking back, how proud I am of this association of distinguished painters, whose level of

Dee Beard Dean

Island Living
oil on canvas
20 x 20 inches

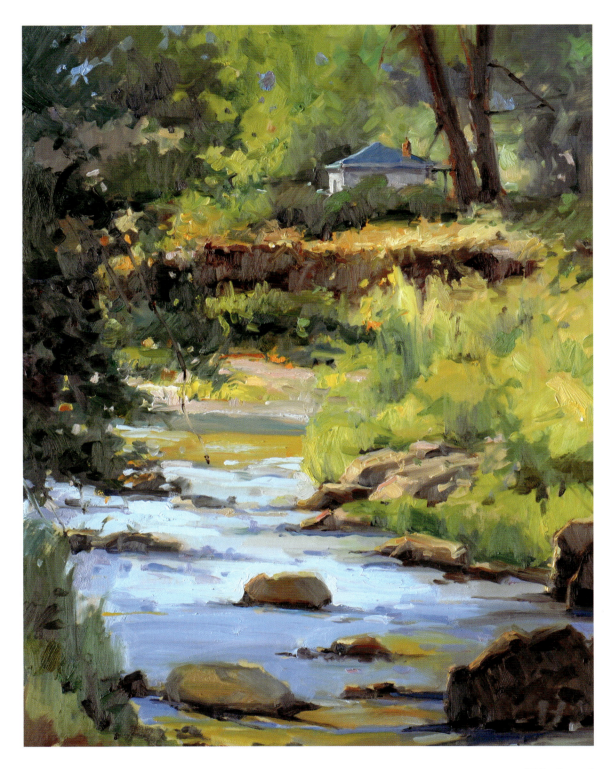

Elk Creek
oil on canvas
30 x 24 inches

excellence has made this group one of the top *plein air* organizations in the country. From its inception, Plein Air Painters of the Southeast (PAP-SE) maintained high standards of excellence. Now this group enjoys national recognition and a growing demand for their artworks and workshops."

From PAP-SE's first exhibition, held in Charleston, South Carolina in 2001, the collective talent of this group was apparent. Art collectors, museums and gallery directors began to seek out the works of these Southern painters. To gain increasing recognition, the Plein Air Painters of the Southeast created the website pap-se.com and at least once a year, they conduct a workshop and art exhibition. The spring show consists of three days of *plein air* painting workshops by the members and a final gallery show featuring their larger studio paintings and wet-paint canvases from the week's paint-out demonstrations.

Though the members make their homes in the Southeastern states, wanderlust is a common characteristic among the group. Like Dee's own body of works, the paintings of PAP-SE artists reflect a romance with far-flung cultures, landscapes and architecture, in addition to their provincial love for the unique character of the Southeast with its maritime and mountain forests, its coastal sand dunes and historical Southern charm.

Just as Dee had organized the fellowship of painters she had envisioned, and as this organization, PAP-SE, was garnering greater recognition in the art world, the most difficult trial of Dee's life began. Her husband, David Dean, was diagnosed with cancer.

David had been ill periodically for 12 years before the doctors finally found the cancer. During this time, Dee would paint furiously between his bouts of illness and frequently spend hours on the Internet at night researching his symptoms.

Lowcountry Morning
oil on canvas
30 x 40 inches

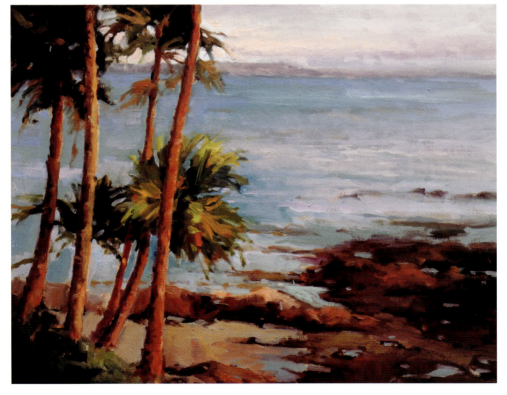

Windy Palms
oil on canvas
20 x 24 inches

Kiawah Island Marsh
oil on canvas
24 x 24 inches

Kiawah Marsh Wetlands
oil on canvas
16 x 20 inches

A Painter By Providence

Noon Tide
oil on canvas
20 x 24 inches

Dee Beard Dean

Grandfather Mountain (LEFT)
oil on canvas
24 x 30 inches

Through her online research, Dee was able to connect one of his vague symptoms (a pain in his shoulder) with liver cancer. She convinced the doctors to do the tests and the cancer was finally detected, only too late.

Toward the end of his life, Dee's full-time job was giving care to her husband who was debilitated by the spreading cancer. "Looking back, I count it a calling and a privilege to have helped him through his final months," recalls Dee.

She remembers with gratitude how "David proudly supported my work, giving me encouragement and often making frames for my paintings. I wasn't able to paint for some time after he passed away. I had to heal and sort out my life emotionally. Eventually, I was able to focus on creating art again."

People often intuitively turn to art or some other creative endeavor to sustain them in times of trauma or emotional healing. Sometimes the satisfaction of creating art can act as a cure to tragedy and loss by tapping the deep reservoirs of strength in the human spirit and also calling attention to the cherished gifts of life bundled into every passing moment.

Dee Beard Dean

A Painter By Providence

Sunset Sail
oil on canvas
30 x 40 inches

Dee Beard Dean

Ecuadorian Woman
oil on canvas
40 x 30 inches

ambassadors of art

As Dee has discovered in her trips around the world, art has a most unique power to unite people through their common hopes, dreams and inspirations. She feels that art—like music and other art forms—can bring a much-needed sense of peace and unity to a troubled world. Every trip she now embarks upon only reinforces this view.

Shortly after moving to North Carolina, Dee met Dr. Nicolai Chalfa in January 2006. With a mutual love of art and travel, Dee and Nick became instant soul mates and a year later they married. The hand of fate that brought them together quickly waved them off on journeys around the world in search of new subjects to paint and explore.

Dee and Nick first traveled to Ecuador in 2007 to visit two men who had once lived with Nick and his family as exchange students forty-five years ago. Nick and one of the Ecuadorian men stayed in touch through the decades though they had not seen each other again, until this visit. Nick and Dee stayed with this longtime friend on his family's balsa tree plantation where balsa wood is grown and exported to markets around the world. With great excitement and pride, they showed their American guests all the modern and indigenous wonders of Ecuadorian villages, cities, mountains and coasts. Nick and Dee saw city streets enlivened with weavers and market vendors. Outside the cities, they watched sheepherders and fisherman eking a living off the bountiful land and coastal waters.

In the beautiful colonial city of Cuenca, Dee and Nick were introduced to the local foods, and tried their taste buds on cuy (pronounced "cooey"), which is roasted guinea pig. These animals are raised for consumption the way Americans raise chickens. Both Dee and Nick fell in love with the mannerism and traditional garb of the Indian tribes, especially those of the native women whose fashion statements included tall Panama hats and colorful, hand-dyed pleated skirts that flipped up at the hemline as they walked sprightly down the streets. Their hair braids and hand-woven shawls were worn in distinctive ways to indicate whether a woman was married or single. The Panama hats, which were specific to the tribe or region to which the women belonged, were originally men's fashion. As the story goes, Dee and Nick learned that a ship arrived with a container of these hats long ago and the women, with their short, stout build but proud demeanor, had donned the hats to make themselves look taller.

During one afternoon's trip to Cuenca, Dee and her husband visited the city's Museum of Modern Art and had the opportunity to meet the museum director. Nick, in his fluent Spanish, explained to the director that Dee was a well-known artist from America. He handed the director Dee's card as they said good-bye. Several months passed, and the couple received an e-mail from the museum director who, having viewed Dee's website, expressed a strong interest in having a show of her works at the museum. Dee happily agreed.

The invitation sparked an idea between Dee and Nick. They began dreaming of the possibility of arranging group shows in Ecuador involving nationally known American artists for the mutual exchange of art and ideas across the continents. "Much of what

A Painter By Providence

Laundry Day in San Miquel
oil on canvas
16 x 20 inches

Dee Beard Dean

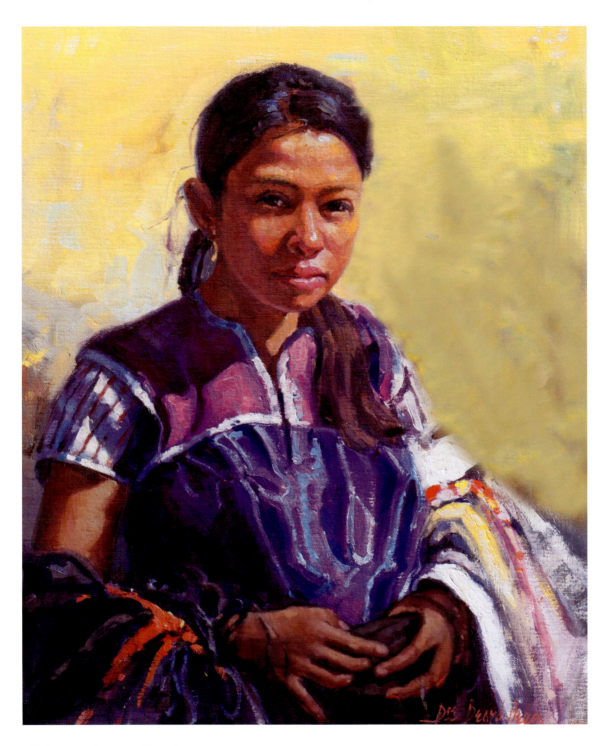

Chiapas Street Vendor
oil on canvas
24 x 20 inches

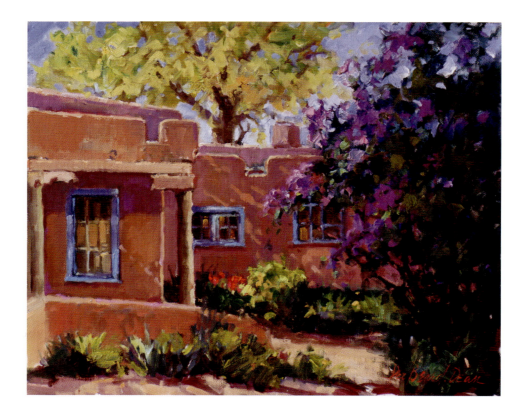

The Blumenschein Museum
oil on canvas
16 x 20 inches

we know about the great works of art from other countries we learn from biographical books and museum works of their Old Masters. It occurred to me that countries have so much to learn from each other's contemporary artists and that more effort should be made to bring together living artists from the far regions of the world," explains Dee.

Their Ecuadorian experience left Dee and Nick with a feeling that there exists a wide world of opportunity for artists of all nations to share their talents, knowledge and artistic traditions with each other, not unlike the concept of university exchange students. Artists could tour a host country and become immersed, for a while, in the country's language, culture, museums and art academies. Nick and Dee returned from their South American travels with a new mission to explore ways of encouraging the global outreach of international artists and their masterful works.

With this future mission in mind, they hope to organize "exchanges" of notable artists, and conduct art exhibitions and demonstrations with other countries, beginning with Dee's exhibition in Ecuador. "Art is the universal language, so it seems a logical beginning to unite people from around the world to share knowledge and, in some cases, promote compassion for the plight of less fortunate people." Dee relates, "In my travels, I am constantly reminded how blessed we Americans are for our prosperity and freedom of opportunity. In Mexico, I became acquainted with a young girl named Veronica who sold dolls to tourists on the street until late at night. She belonged to a family of doll makers and she had an almost angelic spirit and such a delightful, precocious personality. Still, I often wonder what will become of that child. Will she be able to grow up safe and will she ever have the opportunities she so deserves in life beyond selling dolls on a street corner?"

Dee completed a painting titled "The Dollmakers" which was her way of both honoring their artisan traditions and offering American art lovers a vignette of these Mexican families and their simple, handcrafted lifestyle. Dee also continues to paint many figures of Ecuadorian women sporting their panama hats and traditional garb.

Sadly, it was clear to Nick and Dee that the old way of life in some of these countries is rapidly disappearing. Even in third-world countries, so far removed from American cities, our Western influence is replacing many of the traditional lifestyles of native peoples. Dee recalls how in Cuenca and elsewhere, mothers and daughters

Sketch of Veronica
oil on canvas
12 x 9 inches

would walk together down the street, yet look as if they were from separate cultures: the mother in her colorful traditional dress and the daughter in Western-style jeans and T-shirts.

Scenes such as this call attention to the bleak prediction that in one or two more generations, American artists like Dee might never see the colorful and unfamiliar street scenes or the untouched beauty of other countries. Rather the world seems poised to become a homogenous reflection of North American and European cities. "It's heartbreaking that so many traditional lifestyles are changing and disappearing. The way of life in many countries seem so rich in family camaraderie and so much happier and relaxed than American lifestyles. For instance, in San Miguel, whole families would walk to the town center every evening to visit together and watch the children play. And in Bordeaux, France, people would close up shop at 4:00 p.m. to socialize in street cafes. As an artist, I feel it's important to capture these authentic scenes while they still exist."

Dee's evolution as a professional artist—with its unlikely beginning in the rural countryside of Indiana, and often fortuitous turn of events—seemed mapped out by the hand of fate. In contrast to Veronica, the Mexican doll seller, Dee's earliest years were full of opportunities, which she characteristically and eagerly embraced. Dee's approach to life and career have been, above all, bold. And, as the Scottish mountaineer W.H. Murray tells us, "boldness has genius, magic and power in it."

Cuenca Indian Woman (LEFT)
oil on canvas
40 x 30 inches

English Morn II
oil on canvas
12 x 30 inches

Though hers has been a life of golden opportunities, it was certainly not without its attendant troubles. Yet, Dee's talent and her love of art kept her grounded in positive ideals, and satisfied and self-assured enough to tackle any issue. "Problems can destroy you or strengthen you," relates Dee, "I just always chose to be strengthened by them."

Art was the motivating and healing force in her life but an abiding faith in God provided the unshakable foundation for her inner strength. Whenever problems arose, she never felt they would destroy her life or happiness because she never felt alone. And she knew that between God's ever-present grace and her own creative problem-solving abilities, she would always have the help she needed. "In addition to painting, I have found that writing my thoughts down on paper also helped both my creative process and spiritual growth. Journaling allowed me to turn my problems over to God and fostered healing from past wounds," comments Dee.

Dee has reached a point in her career and life where she has learned to be protective of her sense of joy and energy. Instead of dwelling on hardships or pain, she simply observes the world through trained and attuned eyes, then she picks up a brush and she paints.

Close to Home
oil on canvas
16 x 20 inches

Like the passages of Dee's life, her body of works reveal an artist bursting with energy and enthusiasm for everything under the sun. In the lush, textured swipes of pigment on canvas, her brushstrokes express an emotional depth and wide-open joy borne of standing out in the cool of countless mornings, painting shadows swimming in the ripples of a pond or blue-tinged mountains set aglow by the rising sun.

For Dee Beard Dean, life is about purpose, and creating art is her path to living every day with elegance and mindful intention. Scenes painted in homage to the Creator and to the beauty of His creation are Dee's way of reciprocating for a lifetime of wonderful memories and simple blessings. Her body of works radiate, at once, a highly disciplined mastery of tool and pigment and a joyful, unbridled abandon in embracing the magical beauty of light falling on form.

DEE BEARD DEAN

Mountain Road
oil on canvas
11 x 14 inches

A PAINTER BY PROVIDENCE

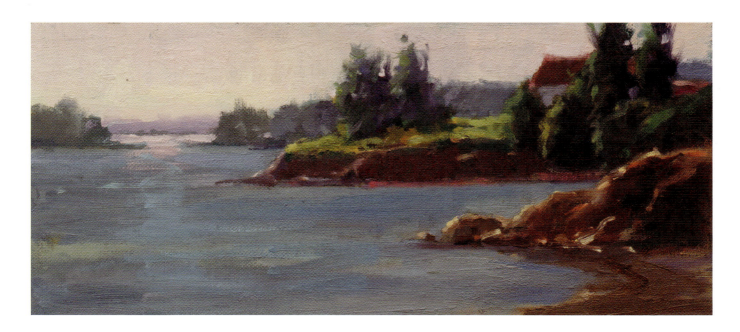

Before Dusk
oil on canvas
12 x 24 inches

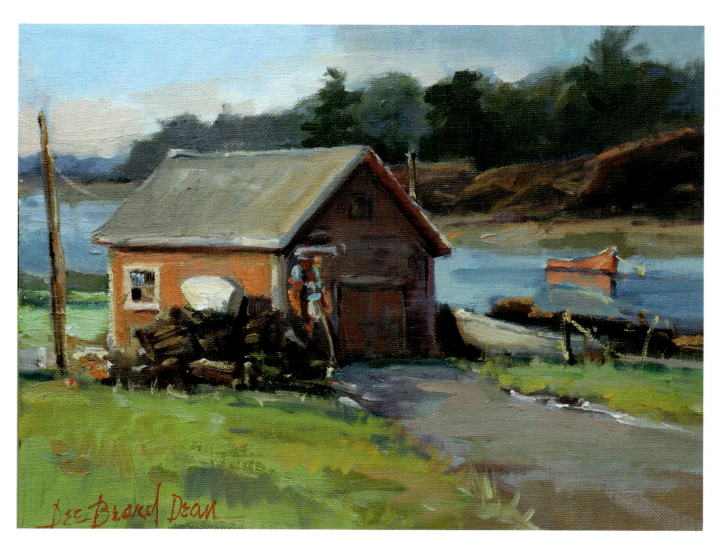

Red Rowboat
oil on canvas
11 x 14 inches

John's Island Morning
oil on canvas
11 x 14 inches

DEE BEARD DEAN

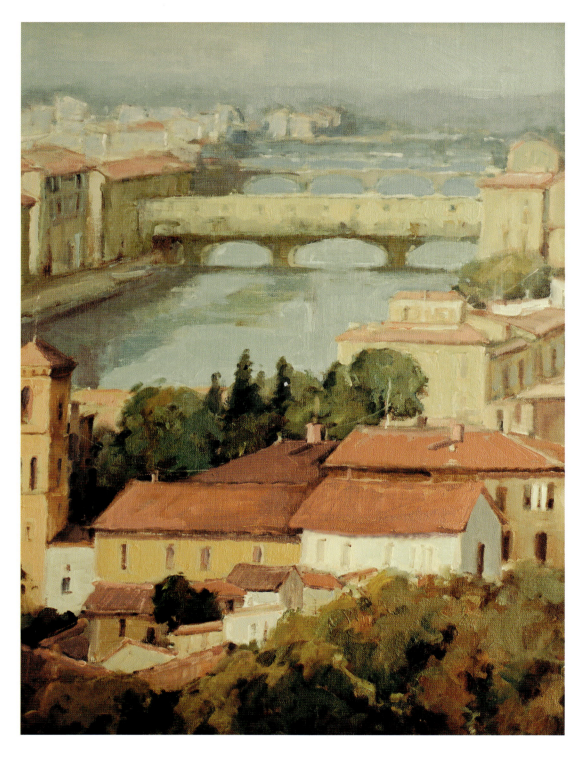

Fiume Arno River
oil on canvas
30 x 24 inches

index

aerial perspective   *84*
alla prima   *89*
Amish   *22, 26*
art
  "art girl"   *22*
  academic principals   *30*
  art school   *30*
  career choice   *33*
  connoisseurs and collectors   *143*
  driftwood art   *40, 43*
  galleries   *21*
art demons   *112*
artistic
  aptitude   *29*
  drive   *29*
  experimentation   *84*
  self-discipline   *63*
  versatility   *104*
artistic spirit, soul   *22, 110*
art, memory and emotion   *76*
Athens, Georgia   *83, 140*
Atlanta, Georgia   *69, 70*
Atlanta Portrait Society   *70*

Bass, Clayton   *13*
Barker, Dolores   *22*
Beverly Hills, California   *58*
Bohemian dream   *43*
Bordeaux, France   *163*
business and marketing skills   *63*

cancer   *146, 151*
Cape Cod School of Art   *89, 101*
cave drawings   *140*
Cessna 150 airplane   *60*
Chalfa, Dr. Nick   *134, 155*
Charleston, South Carolina   *146*
color contrasts   *97*
color harmony   *103*
colorist movement   *89*

Costa Rica   *134*
Cowboy Quick Draw   *120*
creative
  self-expression   *29, 108, 112*
  spirit   *108, 110*
  void   *108*
Cuenca, Ecuador   *156, 160*
Cuenca Museum of Modern Art   *156*
cuy (guinea pig)   *156*

Dean, David   *146*
Dee Beard Collections label   *58, 60, 61*
Dee Beard Dean (see Barker, Dolores)   *21, 22*
  children—Terry and John   *39, 40*
  siblings—Bonnie, Don, Jerry, Jim   *22*
Dee's Boutique   *55*
discouragement   *108*

Ecuador   *155, 156, 160*
energize a canvas   *112*
England   *76*
en plein air   *83, 84, 104, 143, 146*
European designs   *56*
Everglades   *55*

Famous Artists School   *30*
  TV fashion expert   *63*
fashion industry   *63, 69*
fear of failure   *64, 110*
fine art   *63*
Florida Keys
  Everglades   *55*
  Florida Bay   *39*
  Key Largo shanties   *46*
  Old Conch culture   *43*
  relocating   *39*
  roseate spoonbills   *46*
  spider monkeys   *39*
focal points   *104*
France   *134, 163*

French Impressionism *84*
Ft. Myers, Florida *55, 56, 63*
fundamentals of art *107*

Galleria Specialty Mall *69*
global outreach, international artists *160*
God, faith in *133, 164, 165*
gray goods *58*
Greece *134*
Gruppé, Emile *89, 90*
Gulf Coast, Florida *55*

hair braids *156*
hand-dyed pleated skirts *156*
harmonious color palettes *58*
harmonious grays *91*
Hawthorne, Charles Webster *89, 103*
healing *76, 151, 164*
Henri, Robert *107*
Hensche, Henry *89*
host of fashion segment *63*

illusion of reality *83*
impressionistic brushstrokes *83*
impressionistic palette *46*
Impressionistic Realist *97*
Impressionists *84, 89, 90, 97*
Indiana *22, 26, 30, 46, 104, 163*
invention of paint tubes *89*
Italy *134*

journaling *164*

Kendall School of Art and Design *33*

La Grange News *140*
Laguna Beach, California *143*
Leatherwood Mountains, North Carolina *120*
learning curve *107*
likeness *70, 73, 83*
living memory *75*
luminosity *97, 133*

Marathon, Florida *43*
Merrick, Peggy *43*
Mexico *134, 160*
Miami, Florida *39, 55*
motivation *64*
mural *30*
Murray, W. H. *163*
muted colors *90*

Nagel, Gwen *83*
Naples, Florida *60*
nature versus nurture debate *29*
negotiating skills *63*
Netherlands *90*
New American label *60*
New American logo *63*
New England *90*
North Carolina *69, 155*

Old Masters *159*
open-air painter *133*
Orlando, Florida *58*
outdoor moment *97*
Outdoor Painter's Forum *120*

painting workshops *101, 112*
paint-out demonstration *121*
Panama hats *156, 160*
pen-and-ink sketches *56*
persona and personality *70*
plein air painters *119, 143*
Plein Air Painters of America (PAPA) *143*
Plein Air Painters of the
    Southeast (PAP-SE) *120, 146*
plein air painting workshops *146*
portfolio *69*

portrait commissions *43, 70, 75, 76*
portraiture *43, 83*
Portugal *140*
Prêt-à-Porter *60*
principles of landscape painting *112*
protégé *43*

Provincetown, Massachusetts   *89*

retail marketing   *55*
rock people   *40*
runway shows   *58, 63*

San Miguel, Mexico   *134, 163*
Santayana, George   *134*
sewing and patternmaking skills   *56, 58*
soft grays   *90, 94*
Southeastern United States   *101, 143, 146*
Southern charm   *146*
Southern painters   *146*
Spain   *140*
spiritual mission   *140*
Strickland, George   *104, 143*

Tavernier, Florida   *39*
The Art Spirit,   *107*
traditional lifestyles, native peoples   *163*

unstoppable determination   *112*
unveiling   *76*

Veronica   *160, 163*

www.pap-se.com   *146*
Western influence   *160*
wet paint shows   *146*
work ethic   *26*
Worth Avenue, Palm Beach Florida   *58*